SOCIALISE

SOCIALISE

Unlock your content, maximise social media engagement and win more work than ever before

**IAIN SCOTT
REBECCA HOLLOWAY
CHARLIE STEWART**

Copyright © Base Creative UK Ltd., 2023

All rights reserved

Edition 1.1

No part of this book may be reproduced in any written, electronic, recording, or photocopying without written permission of the publisher or author. The exception would be in the case of brief quotations embodied in the critical articles or reviews and pages where permission is specifically granted by the publisher or author/authors.

Although every precaution has been taken to verify the accuracy of the information contained herein, the author and publisher assume no responsibility for any errors or omissions. This book is not intended to provide personalised legal or financial advice. No liability is assumed for damages that may result from the use of information contained within.

Cover image © Base Creative UK Ltd.

FOREWORD

By Andy Lambert

Social media isn't about going viral.

In marketing, we're always at risk of becoming obsessed with numbers. Every day there's a new way to measure data and a new piece of technology. As technology changes, however, I'm a strong believer that human connection will be increasingly essential to businesses that want to stand out and grow.

Storytelling is one of the most impactful - and human - marketing tools at our disposal. Sharing stories helps brands engage with their audiences on a deeper level. They compel people to connect with a brand's mission, its values and purpose. Storytelling doesn't just spark curiosity, it invites people to be part of a larger narrative.

We're emotional beings, and marketing that evokes emotion is incredibly powerful. We seek belonging and connection. When brands understand their audiences' desires, fears, and aspirations, they can create campaigns that fill us with emotion, fostering communities by bringing people together around shared interests, values, and passions. Whether it's joy, nostalgia or inspiration, emotions make marketing messages memorable, drive action and create a sense of belonging.

Socialise understands the power of social media storytelling and how it can transform your marketing by tapping into our emotions and desire for belonging and connection. It hits that sweet spot between big picture principals and the kind of practical advice you can apply everyday as you construct a story-driven social media marketing campaign.

If you're going to stand out and win more work, human connections need to drive your social media marketing. If you're ready to take that leap, *Socialise* is the book for you.

- Andy Lambert, Founding Team and Director of Growth at ContentCal, sold to Adobe

CONTENTS

INTRODUCTION 11
   The authors 18
PART 1 21
   You have what you need 21
   The power of storytelling 22
   Social animals 31
PART 2 39
   Creating your
   social media strategy 39
   Setting smart goals 41
   Targeting the right audience
   and channel 53
   Original, valuable, shareable content 71
   How to tell stories 81
   Attracting your audience and maintaining relationships 99
   Influencing influencers 110
   Measuring success 119
PART 3 133
   Telling your stories
   on social media 133
   Q&A sessions 135
   Promoting thought leadership 142

    Talent acquisition... 148
    Promoting events..152
    Technical writing..154
    Lead generation..155
    Influencers and brand ambassadors................................. 160
    ESG content.. 163
    Investor relations.. 170
    User-generated content...172
CLOSING & THANKS...181
    So what's next?... 181
    References... 182
    Acknowledgements... 183
    Thank You... 184

INTRODUCTION

The statistics are staggering.

Social media use is growing in double digits[A]. Over half of the world's population is on social media, and over 90% of internet users use at least one social media platform.

Even as some social platforms approach their 20th birthdays, research continues to show that social media marketing is booming. It also continues to change. Image and video-based posts are now over 40x more likely to be shared than posts without a visual element, and over 90% of brands that post videos on social media get new customers[B].

There's just one problem.

If social media marketing is bigger than ever, why isn't it working for you and your campaigns?

You post images and videos and get some engagement, but nowhere near the level it deserves.

When you look through your professional social media feed, other people's posts get hundreds of likes, shares and comments. Your posts - or those you post for your company - only attract a handful of reactions mainly from work colleagues who've probably been asked to engage.

Before we delve into why that is, try this. Find your most successful social media post. It could be on any platform, professional or personal. Literally look back. Open up the app, review your posts over the past year and find that stand-out success.

You probably thought of one specific post right away. You remembered the feeling when all those likes, comments and reactions came flooding in. The immediate rush, the slight lull, then the second wave. Then, when you checked at the end of the week, you saw the number of engagements had doubled.

Find *that* post. Read it, remember it. We'll be relying on it later.

For me, there are two posts. Both were on a social media platform I predominantly use to connect and interact with my professional network, LinkedIn.

The first was written on my 40th birthday as a way of celebrating my rollover into a new decade. In the post, I recalled what had motivated me to start a digital marketing agency 16 years before, and the journey I'd been on reciting its challenges and its achievements.

The second post was written after a cycling accident I was involved in, that led to a broken arm, dislocated elbow and a trip to A&E. It was a post about gratitude. It highlighted the help, support and attention I received from members of the public, from the police, medics, paramedics and private security whose involvement completely changed the outcome of the accident.

Both posts had approximately 5 times more engagement than my other posts on the same platform.

What was it about these posts that led to such high engagement? Why these posts over all others?

First, it's worth acknowledging the posts that get a relatively *low level* of engagement. You know the kind.

"I'm excited to announce that our firm has…"

"At XYZ company, we're passionate about growing your business into…"

"ABC Limited is proud to welcome David to the team…"

You've probably written a few posts like those yourself. Don't worry, we all have. Just as it's important to know why some posts succeed, it's important to know why other posts flop.

Usually, people point to the subject matter: 'no one really cares what your firm has done', 'everyone and every business is passionate about something', and 'people come and go from companies all the time - who cares?'

But pointing to the *subject matter* as the culprit would be a mistake. It isn't the subject matter that makes the difference between a successful post and an unsuccessful one. Think of it like a joke. If a joke isn't funny, it's rarely because of the subject matter, but because of how the subject matter is dealt with or communicated. It's about how the joke is told.

The big difference between a successful post and an unsuccessful one is *storytelling*.

Your content isn't boring. You're just communicating your content in a boring way.

This isn't a book about storytelling *theory,* however. There are plenty of fantastic books dedicated to the art of storytelling and how to craft a believable setting, build suspense and bring everything to a satisfying resolution.

This also isn't a book about big-budget story-based ad campaigns either. It won't tell you how to create the next Oxo family, the super-successful advert characters who sold gravy granules in the 1980s[C]. Nor will it help create a 21st century version of the Nescafe "Gold Blend" romance that sold coffee in the 90s[D].

This book is dedicated to helping you understand how to use powerful *storytelling methods* for your social media content in the corporate world - for every day content, without spending millions.

This book focuses on a fundamental part of human nature: we all love sharing great stories with as many people as we can. By adapting your social media content to use this powerful *shareability* strategy, you'll see a dramatic change in the reactions and responses from your followers.

If you follow the lessons in this book, you won't need to spend any more time or money than you're already doing. You won't need to create complicated spreadsheet formulas or download yet another social media software product.

In Part 1 of *Socialise*, you will learn why storytelling is so powerful, and how the right kind of stories can transform dry information into trusted beliefs.

In Part 2, you will learn how to take stories and apply them to a measurable, goal-based framework - your social media marketing campaign. You will learn how to better manage your current campaigns to gain higher engagement and acquire a more qualified following.

In Part 3, you will find examples of social media storytelling techniques applied to a range of goals and situations so that you're left in no doubt about how to take your social media to the next level, no matter the context.

This book will equip you with the tools and techniques to tell stories on any social media platform, from those that have been around since the mid 2000s to those that are yet to be created. The underlying principles laid out in *Socialise* don't depend on flashy new features and widgets.

Everything you need, you already have.

Everything you need to do, humans have been doing for thousands of years.

As you journey through this book, you'll discover that while the ideas can be applied at campaign level, they work most powerfully when used day-to-day. They're most effective when you make them the norm, the de facto method as you create *all* your sales and marketing content.

Then, you'll begin to see the rewards and further applications beyond social media, through channels like email marketing, blog and website articles, and (for those that do) in the way you pitch for new work.

Once you've read this book (and we suggest you read this more than once), you'll be able to instinctively apply its lessons to your social media marketing strategy, wherever you work, whatever the campaign and whatever the objectives.

While others still believe that buying likes and paying for comments is the way to go, you'll be able to rely on techniques that attract genuine engagement. You won't just get one like a day, or a couple of comments a week. You'll see a qualified and engaged following grow around your content like you've never seen before - a following that can be leveraged time and time again on future campaigns that will ultimately drive the right kind of behaviour to positively impact your organisation's bottom line.

Social media is sometimes seen as a drab necessity - a box-ticking exercise, especially for professional service firms, B2B and corporate communications. "We need to post because we need to be present." It's wrongly seen as simple brand awareness.

You're reading this book because you want to change that. You want to create impactful social media content that transcends necessity, and becomes an integral part of a "buyer journey" that's pivotal to every campaign you're involved in.

Done well, your social media content will send a positive ripple through every other marketing activity. You'll support the company's SEO, leading to greater visibility in search engines. You'll help to reduce the cost-per-click on your Google Ad campaigns, maximising campaign budgets. You'll gain more signups to your company's newsletter. You'll build trust and loyalty among potential buyers - those that your organisation's sales team will eventually pitch to. You'll make the sales team's job exponentially easier and quicker.

Socialise will enable you to meet your marketing objectives, grow a following, encourage engagement and win more work than ever before.

- Iain Scott, founder and CEO of Base Creative

The authors

Iain Scott is the founder and CEO of Base Creative, with 20 years of experience in the digital marketing industry. He is the author of the book *50 Days of Social Media* and co-host of the podcast *Sharing Social*. Iain is a guest lecturer at City University, sharing his knowledge of digital marketing with the next generation of marketing professionals. His expertise has seen him invited as the recurring host of BrightonSEO's Paid Social Show, introducing industry leaders from around the world.

Iain was already running an agency when Twitter and Facebook were created. He's the first to admit that he initially resisted social marketing. However, as he began to understand why it was working, he realised that this new tool was using an age-old technique - tapping into our storytelling instincts.

Today, Iain is on a mission to harness the good that social media can bring and to use it to empower the world, his organisation and his clients. With his vast knowledge and experience, Iain is leading the way in the digital marketing industry and helping businesses to succeed in the ever-changing world of social media.

linkedin.com/in/iaingscott

Rebecca Holloway is an award-winning Senior Social Media Strategist at Base Creative. With 10 years of experience in the digital marketing industry, she has made waves in the social media world. She co-hosts the *Sharing Social* podcast with Iain, and has been recognized for her outstanding achievements, winning the

Digital Women Awards' *Young Digital Woman of the Year 2021* and *Social Media Manager of the Year 2022*.

Rebecca is a guest lecturer at the Alt Marketing School and the co-host for the *Alt Marketing School Podcast*. A sought-after speaker, she has been invited to talk at the BrightonSEO Paid Social Show four times, as well as at Digital Women, and Cambridge Social Media Meetup.

Rebecca grew up with social media, but it was during her apprenticeship that she saw the medium take off for businesses, leading her to specialise in social media marketing. She has witnessed the birth of new platforms like TikTok and pioneered its use in marketing campaigns. Her highly successful campaign for the organisation Young Scot was featured as an early example of TikTok marketing on the platform's creative centre. She has seen businesses become more and more open to social media - and how they reap the rewards.

linkedin.com/in/beccasocial

Charlie Stewart is a Content Strategist at Base Creative, helping colleagues and clients harness the power of storytelling across their content and social media marketing every day. With a background as a writer, editor, and publicist, he brings his creative flair to content and copy across search, web and social media campaigns.

Charlie has built a vast array of creative and communications skills, including animating and video editing, consulting on video game design, producing podcasts and theatre and penning hundreds of articles. These mediums all have their own storytelling techniques - Charlie's job is to unlock them.

A background in sales also gives him a unique insight into the needs and wants of customers, allowing him to create content that resonates with target audiences and drives engagement. As he looks to the future of digital marketing, Charlie's breadth of storytelling experiences prepares him to find new storytelling opportunities wherever they arise.

linkedin.com/in/charlieastewart

PART 1

You have what you need

"Stories constitute the single most powerful weapon in a leader's arsenal."

— Dr. Howard Gardner, developmental psychologist, Harvard University

In Part 1 of this book, you will learn about the power of storytelling, and how the right kind of stories can turn dry information into trusted beliefs.

Our social hardwiring led to the development of the storytelling instincts that social media amplifies to this day - you can use those instincts to build and influence your audience.

Let's get started.

The power of storytelling

"I've learned that people will forget what you said, people will forget what you did, but people will never forget how you made them feel."

— Maya Angelou, writer and activist

It's 1983. Steve Jobs has just launched Apple's second line of desktop computers. It's been a disaster.

The Apple Lisa sold just 10,000 units in two years. To Apple's board of directors, this made no sense. The Lisa was pushing the envelope. Its technical feats were acclaimed. Many of its innovative features would quickly become industry standards.

Despite the high price (nearly $10,000) Steve Jobs was confident that the Lisa's advanced features would speak for themselves and win businesses over. He was wrong. The technicalities went over the audience's head. They were being told something, but they couldn't imagine how it would make them *feel*.

One year later, Apple launched the Macintosh. Its hardware was less advanced than the Lisa's. It had less RAM, a lower-resolution display and no hard disk drive support. On paper, it was the inferior machine.

By May 1984, the Macintosh had sold 70,000 units.

Why?

The power of storytelling.

The failed Apple Lisa launched with magazine ads that put its impressive innovations front and centre. They included taglines like "it took 200 years to develop programs you can learn in 20 minutes." After the Lisa flopped, Jobs took a very different approach to Apple's marketing at the Macintosh product launch in 1984,

"It is 1958," he began. "IBM passes up the chance to buy a young, fledgling company that has invented a new technology called xerography. Two years later Xerox is born. IBM has been kicking themselves ever since."

This dramatic start set the scene for an ambitious feat of storytelling that would transform Apple's fortune. Jobs cast IBM - known in the industry as Big Blue - as the evil, monopolising monster set to swallow up the industry. Only Apple stood in its way, protecting the computer market's "future freedom."

Steve Jobs had become a convert to the power of storytelling, and a zealous one at that.

The Macintosh flew off the shelves.

He left Apple to found his own storytelling company - Pixar. When he returned to Apple in 1997, his honed storytelling style would become key to the success of the iPod, the iPhone and the iPad. His legendary product launches drew Apple's audience into carefully crafted narratives. There were villains. There were heroes. There were battles between freedom and tyranny, good and evil.

By the time any product itself was being shown, the audience had come to their own conclusion, one Jobs' storytelling had been leading them to all along. The Lisa's disastrous launch had taught him a vital lesson.

Stop writing information. Start writing stories.

Steve Jobs might have mastered this craft in the age of personal computers, but humans have been harnessing the power of storytelling for thousands of years.

Think of some of the first stories you heard as a child. Fables and fairy tales are packed full of information, designed to take advantage of the human brain's innate attraction to stories.

Here's one of the most common stories told to American children. There are many different versions, but they all go something like this:

> Once upon a time, there lived a farmer and his son. When the boy turned six years old, his father decided to gift him an axe.
>
> The boy began hacking away at everything he could get his hands on. Kindling? Hacked. Wheat? Hacked. Pea plants? Tree vines? Flowers? Hacked, hacked, hacked.
>
> In his garden, the farmer had a prized cherry tree. He was on his morning walk one day when, to his horror, he saw that the tree had been chopped down. The farmer fetched his son.

"Do you know who chopped down my cherry tree?" he asked. The boy braced himself.

"Father, I cannot tell a lie. I cut down the tree."

To the boy's surprise, his father hugged him. "Your honesty is worth more to me than a thousand cherry trees," he said.

That boy's name was George Washington.

The lesson is simple: great people tell the truth.

If this is the lesson, why the verbose preamble leading up to it? Why not whack that moral on a sign and hang it above the entrance to every pre-school in the USA?

When you give the human brain information *without* telling it a story, you'll struggle to get it to believe you on an emotional level. That was the problem with the Apple Lisa's marketing. Make a lesson the outcome of a story, however, and you can get your audience to trust what you're saying.

The cherry tree story doesn't just *tell* children not to lie. It does something far smarter. It makes them *want* to be honest.

The Lisa's marketing *told* Apple's audience that it was the superior machine. The Mac's marketing made them *want* to be part of a revolution against IBM.

Studies have shown that the George Washington tale is far more effective at getting children to tell the truth than similar stories.

Dr. Kang Lee at the University of Toronto ran an experiment to measure the impact of morality tales on children[1]. When given the opportunity to confess to a lie, children who had been told the cherry tree story were more likely to be honest than children who had been told the stories of *Pinnochio* or *The Boy Who Cried Wolf*. Why?

In the story, George Washington is rewarded for good behaviour. Pinnochio and the boy who cried wolf are punished for bad behaviour. It's no wonder why children who heard *Pinnochio* or *The Boy Who Cried Wolf* didn't want to own up.

Stories are extremely powerful tools, but exactly how a story is told can have a huge impact on whether or not it changes an audience's behaviour. Each of those stories told children not to lie, but only one used the right techniques to make them more honest. Again - it's about getting your audience to *want* something.

Instruct your audience without using a good story that gets their wants to align with yours, and you'll find it far harder to get them to believe you.

If your audience doesn't believe you, it doesn't matter if you're right.

When the storyteller understands their audience's wants, fables and fairy tales help turn instructions into beliefs.

Although you grow out of children's stories, you never stop being vulnerable to the power of narratives. How many presentations begin with the phrase "I'd like to start with a story"?

This chapter begins with a story about Steve Jobs designed to get you to believe in the power of storytelling. You've probably already noticed some of the techniques it uses.

It begins with a surprising hook which relates to a famous, successful figure, someone you probably admire or are at least interested in. You *want* the same success they enjoyed. Then, you're led through a highly narrativised version of something that person experienced and learned from.

Often with stories like these, you begin anticipating the lesson before the end.

A good story helps the reader to come to conclusions before it's over.

This is a huge part of the power of storytelling. A good story will have the listener or reader thinking through the implications before they're spelled out. As before, storytellers who can do this do so about aligning the audience's wants with what the storyteller wants from them.

Princeton psychology researcher Uri Hasson coined the term "Neural Coupling" to describe the phenomenon which occurs in the brains of engaged audience members when they listen to somebody tell a story[2].

In a scientific experiment aimed at looking into the power of storytelling and memory recall, participants' brains were scanned as they listened to an emotional 15-minute story. They then took a story comprehension and recall test.

The results showed that those volunteers with the best comprehension of the story experienced brain patterns which closely matched those of the original storyteller, allowing them to anticipate the storyteller's next thoughts.

When you tell a great story, you literally synchronise your audience's brainwaves with yours.

That might sound like science fiction, but it's something people experience firsthand all the time. It's exciting to begin anticipating the possible outcomes of a good movie before it's finished. It's satisfying to begin to synchronise with a story - even if the storyteller isn't in the room.

By the end of Steve Jobs' 1984 Macintosh launch speech, he was shouting out questions to the audience. Having led them along using the storytelling building blocks we first hear as children, Jobs was confident that they'd respond in unison with the answers he wanted:

"IBM wants it all and is aiming its guns to its last obstacle to industry control - Apple. Will Big Blue dominate the entire computer industry?"

The audience shouted "no!"

"The entire information age?"

"No!"

"Was George Orwell right?"

"No!"

Stories are your secret weapon.

They have allowed us to pass on otherwise dry, uncomfortable or complicated truths from generation to generation, long before the advent of the written word or the Apple Macintosh.

Steve Jobs became the master of his own story, not just his company's.

He was never an inventor. In fact, Steve Wozniak once said that Jobs "didn't know anything about the inside of a computer" when the duo co-founded Apple in 1976.

Today, however, Jobs is remembered as the brains behind Apple, to the ire of many a computer scientist. In some ways, he was. What Steve Jobs came to understand from the Apple Lisa's failure was how little the facts impact people by themselves without a great story to get the audience onside.

Stories about Steve Jobs remain a favourite among motivational speakers, forum users, and people writing books just like this one. You can find hundreds of anecdotes all over the internet, each designed to impart their own little lessons. Perhaps that is the testament to his true genius.

What's more powerful than telling a great story that wins you more work?

Convincing others to tell your story for you.

Key takeaways

- Storytelling is a very powerful tool.
- They aren't just a powerful way of conveying information - the right stories will make that information far more convincing to your audience.

Social animals

"We are, as a species, addicted to story. Even when the body goes to sleep, the mind stays up all night, telling itself stories."

— Jonathan Gottschall, *The Storytelling Animal: How Stories Make Us Human*

Once upon a time, there was a wild pig and a sea cow.

The duo were inseparable, and lived together in the forest. They loved to race, and could be seen every day running side by side through the undergrowth.

All was well, until one day, during a particularly close contest, the sea cow tripped and hurt his legs.

Sad that his friend could no longer compete, the wild pig carried the sea cow down to the water. There, they could race to their hearts' content, with the wild pig on the land and the sea cow in his new home, where he remains to this day.

The Wild Pig and the Sea Cow is a story told by the Agta, a group of hunter-gatherer peoples in the Philippines. It promotes compassion, cooperation, and the idea that each person has their place in the world no matter what their ability is.

The Agta consider their storytellers the most important people in their society - twice as important as hunters. Why?

Stories build trust. Trust builds social networks.

UCL anthropologist Andrea Migliano and her students interviewed 300 Agta people[3]. Migliano's research found that storytellers were so highly valued because they strengthened their tribes' social networks:

"You need ways of ensuring cooperation in an egalitarian society, and we realised that you could use stories to broadcast the norms that are important to them."

Agta stories promote themes of friendship, cooperation and the importance of equality.

Another Agta story is about a flying ant, who learns that she is no more important than her wing-less sisters. A third story sees the sun (male) and the moon (female) fight until they realise they are equally matched and decide to share the sky.

Without the Agta's storytellers, there would be no shared values or community for the hunters, the doctors or the tribal leaders to participate in. By maintaining group cohesion, storytelling became key to the Agta's survival.

Of course, individual storytellers aren't just thinking of the big picture. Their high status comes with big benefits. Agta storytellers have more children on average, are seen as more desirable and are more likely to be given gifts.

For ambitious members of the community, becoming a storyteller is a no-brainer. However, sharing stories isn't just a means to an end. Science tells us that there's something far more fundamental at play. It's a principle that will be the secret to your success, whether you're a hunter-gatherer or a social media marketer.

Humans love sharing stories.

There's a difference between the long-term benefits of storytelling and the reasons we're driven to share stories.

The physicist Richard Feynman once joked, "physics is like sex: sure, it may give some practical results, but that's not why we do it."

The same applies to storytelling.

When sharing stories, your brain releases oxytocin. Oxytocin is sometimes called "the love hormone"[4].

It is associated with increased feelings of compassion and empathy. It's the hormone that makes you feel connected to other people. It literally builds trust.

It's oxytocin that drives you to action when you've heard a great story. It's why adverts use stories that tug on our heartstrings. It's why those stories continue to work in sales and marketing, even though your rational brain knows you're being sold something. We're compelled to share stories, and stories compel us to act.

You don't eat because you're thinking about the survival of your species, you eat because you're hungry. You're driven to act by your body chemistry, and the release of oxytocin is your chemical reward for sharing stories. It's our body's way of encouraging us to keep using one of our most powerful survival tools.

Human beings have been hunter-gatherers for at least ninety percent of our history[5]. Today, most of our storytelling isn't about survival, but it's still motivated by the same instincts that evolved to help us survive.

From the Agta to Steve Jobs, humans are individually motivated to develop their storytelling skills and in doing so build coherent communities based on shared values. That value could be co-operation during a hunt. It could be buying Apple computers. It could be sharing your next social media post.

But one thing is for sure.

We have always been driven to share stories. The only thing that's changed is how we do it.

We share content and stories with each other all the time. The content that works fulfils three key criteria, whether it's around a campfire, a dinner table or on social media. It needs to be original, valuable and shareable.

- **Original**
  We like to tell stories that others haven't heard before.
- **Valuable**
  We like to tell stories that provide value to the listener by making them laugh, providing a lesson or helping them in another way.
- **Shareable**
  We like to tell the stories that are easy to articulate, comprehend and pass on.

We used to share stories around fires and shared meals. As the first civilisations bloomed, powerful people began telling stories in monuments and through the written word. Storytelling technology crept at a snail's pace over thousands of years, but its hold over people - when it could reach them - was as powerful as ever.

The invention of the printing press allowed storytellers like 16th century reformer Martin Luther to share works with passionate, narrative titles like *Against the Execrable Bull of the Antichrist* to thousands of avid followers across Europe. This new means of sharing stories allowed the Protestant Reformation to be born. The significance of this new technology in sharing his story and winning support wasn't lost on Luther, who said that "printing is the ultimate gift of God and the greatest one."

Fast forward to the 19th century, and new technologies arose from the telegraph to the telephone that made sharing stories even quicker and easier. The 1890s saw the invention of the radio and the birth of early cinema, both transforming the way we told and received stories. The invention of the TV in the 20th century changed storytelling once again. However, as with radio and cinema, most people remained viewers rather than the storytellers themselves.

The invention of the internet near the end of the century saw the rise of email, chat boards, forums, personal websites and more.

Then came social media.

It gave the average person the ability to share their own stories beyond anything humanity had seen before without the need for Pharaohs, preachers, actors or directors to do it for them.

In the 21st century, social media is the quickest and easiest way to share your stories.

Make no mistake. It's not just speed and ease that makes social media the best way to reach your audience.

Storytelling aside, what else makes social media so powerful? What sets it aside from the technology we've mentioned so far as the ultimate tool for 21st century storytellers?

1. **You can learn about your clients and customers, including their preferences and networks.**

    Plenty of social media platforms allow you to see who likes what. Tracking trends is easy and measurable. You can also learn about the businesses, products, brands and activities that they are interested in.

2. **You can reach new audiences, creating meaningful relationships and winning new clients.**

    Not only can you access the networks of people you're already connected to. You can also nurture and initiate relationships, all without having to attend a networking event.

3. **You can provide a service through your social media channels**.

    With instant communication comes instant customer service. You can keep your clients very happy via social media. With the world watching, this will further improve your reputation.

4. **You can build your reputation as an expert**.

    Start sharing original, valuable, shareable content, and

your audience will quickly begin to see you as an expert. With that comes trust and familiarity. This means you'll be at the forefront of their minds when they're ready to buy.

5. **Your marketing activity is more cost effective**.
   Cost effectiveness isn't just about how much money you spend. Marketing takes up your time too. Using social media you can start to see great results without hours of our time or thousands of pounds being spent.

6. **You can measure your activity's effectiveness**.
   There are many ways we can measure the effectiveness of any social media activity, from likes and shares to more in-depth analytics.

7. **Finally, social media is all about the here and now**.
   You can see and observe conversations between industry leaders without having to wait for the next trade show or publication. Best of all, you can be involved in those conversations too, even beginning to steer it. It's all powerful stuff - and you can be a part of it.

Ironically, social media has given us the power to share stories as individuals in a way that humanity has hardly seen since the birth of storytelling itself - after all, it's not like everyone had access to a printing press, a recording booth or their own movie studio.

That's what makes social media so powerful. It isn't just technically brilliant (allowing us to measure the impact of our stories and track our audience down to the fine details), it also gets us back to the fundamentals - individuals sharing stories with one another on a level playing field.

To use the full power of storytelling to amplify your content and win more work, you need to use the most powerful story sharing tool at your disposal.

Social media is by far your most powerful tool for sharing valuable content.

Now, you need to learn how to use it.

Key takeaways

- Stories build trust.
- That trust has been used to build social networks for thousands of years.
- We have always been driven to share stories. The only thing that's changed is how we do it.
- In the 21st century, social media is your most powerful tool for sharing stories.

PART 2

Creating your social media strategy

"If you think you're too small to have an impact, try going to bed with a mosquito in the room."

— Anita Roddick, The Body Shop founder

The difficult thing about storytelling is that, on the individual level, its impact is subjective. Movie executives might count box office returns, but for most people in the audience, the story's success is entirely a matter of opinion.

You need a way to make the success or failure of your social media storytelling measurable. Only then can you continue to develop and fine-tune your stories and reap the rewards of social media. These chapters will take you through everything you will need to know, from how to set the right goals to measuring your results.

We're going to get into the specifics of social media campaign design. However, this book is designed to be evergreen. It is platform agnostic. It won't tell you how to use specific apps, and it doesn't have click-by-click tutorials on publishing content.

Instead, Part 2 aims to get you to grips with the fundamentals that will help you build social media campaigns for any platform - including platforms which haven't been created yet.

After all, the social media world changes fast. Think back to the last few years alone and all the platforms which have risen to prominence and fallen out of favour.

Part 2 will lead you through the principles you need to follow to build a story *and* data-driven strategy in this constantly changing landscape. You will find specific examples and case studies for different *types* of social media platforms (such as video-based platforms, text-based platforms and image-based platforms) in Part 3.

By the end of Part 2, you will have your social media strategy.

Let's dive right in.

Setting smart goals

"The trouble with not having a goal is that you can spend your life running up and down the field and never score."

— Bill Copeland, poet, historian and author

Tudor football was violent. So violent, in fact, that Henry VIII made it illegal[6].

Games would be played across the countryside between entire towns. Instead of a ball, rival mobs chased an inflated pig's bladder that had been blown up and knotted like a balloon.

The ban on football came into effect in 1540, but the sport itself was so chaotic that the law was almost impossible to enforce. Puritan preacher Thomas Elliot decried the "beastly fury and extreme violence" of the beautiful game.

In his *Anatomie of Abuses*, 16th century writer Philip Stubbs described football as a "bloody and murdering practice… sometimes their necks are broken, sometimes their backs, sometimes their legs, sometimes their arms, sometime one part thrust out of joint, sometime another, sometime their noses gush out with blood."[7]

Between 1500 and 1575, more people were killed playing football than in the sport of sword fighting[8].

In theory, you won Tudor football by capturing the "ball" and taking it back to your town. Sometimes, you would win by taking the ball to the *rival* town.

In practice, most games were a free-for-all punch-up left to the last man standing. 300 years later, the newly formed Football Association introduced an innovation that would change the game forever.

Goalposts.

In just a few years football developed into the precise, skillful sport we know today. The chaos had all but disappeared. Strategy, not brute strength, had become the deciding factor of each game.

Why did football transform so quickly?

You can only develop strategy once you have clear goals.

You will already know the importance of setting goals in business, but the story above illustrates how quickly your goals can be forgotten once things kick off. In Tudor football, the players *thought* they had goals, but without clarity things quickly descended into chaos.

If you aren't careful, you can find yourself becoming purely reactive, running with the crowd and losing track of why your business is active on social media to begin with.

To take advantage of the power of storytelling and succeed on social media, you don't just need to set goals. You need to set the right kind of goals.

You need SMART goals.

- **Specific**
- **Measurable**
- **Achievable**
- **Relevant**
- **Timed**

It's likely you've heard of or even put into practice the idea of SMART goals before. The simple and ubiquitous nature of SMART goals make it a great concept to mould your social media objectives around.

Let's put them into practice.

Imagine that you run a graphic design agency.

Your business has a handful of clients who pay you per project. You also have a decent following of 3,750 users on a social media platform that lets you show off your graphic design work.

You want to build your audience on social media, which you measure by your number of followers. By increasing your follower count, you hope to get your business more clients.

Let's turn this into a SMART goal.

- **Specific:** You want to increase your followers on a particular social media platform.
- **Measurable:** You want to increase your followers by 2,500, from 3,750 to 6,250.
- **Achievable:** You already have 3,750 followers, so getting 2,500 more is clearly attainable.

- **Relevant:** You know that your audience already uses this social media platform.
- **Timed:** You're going to achieve this in the next 4 weeks.

Your new SMART goal looks like this:

> **I am going to increase my followers on this social media platform by 2,500 in the next 4 weeks.**

Now that you know what a SMART goal looks like, you can begin to think about the bigger picture. You need to specify your wider business goals, your smaller marketing goals, and, lastly, your specific campaign goals.

- **Business goals:** These include big picture goals like getting more clients, increasing your turnover or employing new staff. They are usually goals that directly impact your bottom line, e.g. increasing conversions and getting more sales.
- **Marketing goals:** These are goals which are focused on building brand awareness, e.g. acquiring 10 new clients in the next 3 months.
- **Campaign goals:** These goals are more specific, and fit into your larger marketing activity, e.g. generating 50 leads or increasing traffic to your website by 25%.

Let's stick with that graphic design agency example. You've already made sure that your marketing goal, building your social media audience, is a SMART goal, but we can get more specific

Your campaign goal is to increase your client base. We can make that goal SMART too.

- **Specific**
  You want to gain more high net worth clients in the city.
- **Measureable**
  You want to take on an additional 10 clients.
- **Achievable**
  You've done your research. You know that 10% of businesses don't work with a graphic design agency but are open to hiring one. Your competitors have already attained this kind of client base. On top of that, you have the time and resources to take on more clients.
- **Relevant**
  You have reached a point in your company where you are ready to grow and make more money.
- **Timed**
  This needs to happen in the next 3 months.

Now, your SMART campaign goal looks likes this:

> **I am going to take on an additional 10 clients in the next 3 months.**

You might not run a graphic design agency in real life, but you will need to define your goals if you want to positively impact your company and acquire more clients using social media marketing.

Here are some more examples of SMART goals from different sectors.

Company: A digital marketing agency

> **We will increase our monthly revenue from our marketing services by 20% within the next six months by expanding our team, improving our marketing processes, and offering more value-added services to our clients.**

Company: A logistics and transportation company

> **We will increase our social media engagement rate by 30% within the next quarter by creating and sharing more engaging content, partnering with influencers in our industry, and running targeted social media ad campaigns.**

Company: A software development company

> **We will increase our customer engagement rate on social media by 40% within the next six months by creating more engaging social media content, responding to customer**

46

> inquiries promptly, and using social media listening tools to understand customer needs.

Company: A B2B e-commerce platform

> **We will increase our monthly revenue from social media marketing by 25% within the next year by creating and sharing more engaging social media content, optimising our social media advertising campaigns, and partnering with relevant social media influencers.**

Company: A cybersecurity firm

> **We will increase our social media following by 50% within the next six months by creating and sharing more educational and engaging social media content related to cybersecurity, running targeted social media ad campaigns, and partnering with relevant cybersecurity influencers on social media.**

By the end of this chapter, you will know what *your* goals need to be.

Unless you want your social media activity to end in chaos like a game of Tudor football, it's time to ask yourself some questions.

What are your business goals, marketing goals and campaign goals?

Let's begin by setting your business goals.

This is about your vision, your audience and your financial gain. Remember, these will underpin all of your marketing activity. When you set your marketing goals, you should be able to refer back to wider business goals to give those marketing goals clear context.

Here are some questions to ask yourself before reaching out to your audience on social media:

1. Do I want to build my reputation and brand awareness?
2. Do I want to increase my website visitors?
3. Do I want people to interact with me or my brand?

Think about these options, decide which one you want to focus on for now, and form a SMART campaign goal around one of those.

Write down your business goals - what is your company's bottom line? What do you want to achieve? Include the financials.

Write down your marketing goals. Then, pick one marketing goal. This could be about reputation, brand awareness, website visitors, or growing an audience.

From there, you can start thinking about and forming your smaller campaign goals.

Never, ever lose sight of your goals.

Bringing it back to our graphic design agency example, your goals might begin to look like this:

- **Business goal**
  You want to grow your graphic design business and increase its income
- **Marketing goal**
  To grow your business, you need to gain more high-end clients
- **Campaign goal**
  To gain more high-end clients, you need to get people to interact with your brand on social media by increasing your follower count by 2,500

Voila! There we have a simple business goal, a marketing goal and a campaign goal.

Here are some examples of business, marketing and campaign goals across the other example companies we talked about earlier in the chapter.

1. **Company**
   A digital marketing agency
   Business goal
   Increase monthly revenue by 20% within the next year
   Marketing goal
   Increase brand awareness by 30% within the next six months
   Campaign goal
   Generate 50 new leads for content marketing services

through a targeted social media ad campaign in the next month

2. **Company**

   A logistics and transportation company

   Business goal

   Increase customer retention rate by 15% within the next year

   Marketing goal

   Increase social media engagement rate by 40% within the next six months

   Campaign goal

   Increase customer reviews on social media by 25% in the next month through a social media review campaign

3. **Company**

   A software development company

   Business goal

   Increase customer satisfaction rating from 80% to 90% within the next year

   Marketing goal

   Increase customer engagement rate on social media by 50% within the next six months

   Campaign goal

   Generate 100 new software development leads through a targeted social media ad campaign in the next month

4. **Company**

   A B2B e-commerce platform

Business goal

Increase monthly revenue by 15% within the next year

Marketing goal

Increase social media following by 30% within the next six months

Campaign goal

Increase sales of a specific product line by 20% through a targeted social media ad campaign in the next month

5. **Company**

    A cybersecurity firm

    Business goal

    Increase revenue from managed cybersecurity services by 20% within the next year

    Marketing goal

    Increase social media awareness of brand by 50% within the next six months

    Campaign goal

    Increase webinar registrations by 30% in the next month through a targeted social media ad campaign

Your business goals, marketing goals and campaign goals need to be SMART if you're going to meet them and measure their success. Take the time with your team to figure out exactly what your goals are before you move forward, and make sure they are Specific, Measurable, Achievable, Relevant and Timed.

"Hang on," you might be thinking, "what does all this have to do with storytelling?" You need to understand the goals of your social media campaign if you're going to figure out which stories to write and who your audience is. Looking back to your goals will also be invaluable for measuring the success of your stories by helping you to turn their success or failure into something that can be judged more objectively - but we'll get to that later.

Once you have your goals, you have completed the first part of your social media strategy.

Key takeaways

- You need a social media strategy to take advantage of the power of storytelling.
- However, you can't have a strategy if you don't understand your goals.
- These will break down into your business goals, your marketing goals and your campaign goals.
- Your goals should be SMART goals - specific, measurable, relevant, achievable and timed.

Targeting the right audience and channel

"The audience is the most revered member of the theatre. Without an audience, there is no theatre."

— Viola Spolin, actor, director and academic

What did *The Man With the Golden Gun*, *The Dukes of Hazzard*, *The Rockford Files* and *Wonder Woman* have in common?

The AMC Matador.

Back in the '70s, that car was plastered across every screen, and no wonder. The name alone tells you everything you need to know - or are supposed to feel - about the Matador.

To the wrong audience, however, that name was about to cause a big problem for the American Motors Corporation.

The Matador's name reflected a delicate balancing act in its marketing. The car was designed for families. Meanwhile, its macho branding was supposed to appeal to the movie-watching men presumed to have the buying power in their household.

On the mainland USA the name worked wonders. In English, the image of a Matador evokes someone strong but skillful, daring but calculated. As a car name it screams both power and control. The problem came when the car was sold in Puerto Rico.

In Spanish, el matador means "the killer."

Not what you want on your mind with your kids in the backseat.

It doesn't matter if you have the right message if you target the wrong audience.

In this chapter, you will learn how to target the right audience on social media. Then, you will learn how to identify the best social media channels to help you meet your goals.

Your current or future client is the most important person in your organisation.

You need to know them inside and out. They are the person you need to tell stories to. Remember the Apple Lisa? The Lisa's launch failed because Apple failed to understand what its audience's priorities were. You need to understand what motivates them and what kind of stories resonate with them.

Before you get to that stage, however, you need to be able to produce social media content that will appeal to your audience on a more surface level. To do that, you need to understand their preferences. You need to know what kind of content they're interested in, how much they like to read, how much time they spend on social media and how they interact with their favourite brands on any given channel.

To start telling successful stories on social media, you need to go deeper - like Apple, you need to understand their *wants*. The more you understand your audience's deepest desires and drives, the more you'll be able to create content that will resonate with them. This principle is as old as storytelling itself.

Before you can really understand how your audience thinks, you first need to know who they are. Gather some of your team together and get some of the basic facts down about your ideal client.

It's time to build your ideal client profile (ICP).

Building an ICP means understanding the *people* inside the type of business you want to become your next client, not just the business itself. Here's how you can build your ICP:

You need to understand your audience's situation.

1. How old are they?
2. What is their gender identity?
3. Where do they live?
4. Do they have a family?

You need to understand your audience's social status.

1. What interests do they have?
2. What do they like to buy?
3. What do they read?
4. Where do they hang out?
5. Do they like to socialise or not?

You need to understand your audience's economic status.

1. Are they a business professional or an individual?

2. Are they decision makers?
3. Do they have disposable income?

You need to understand your audience's social media activity.

1. Do they use social media for leisure or for work?
2. Are they very active or rarely post themselves
3. Do they share other people and brands' posts

You need to understand your audience's experience with your organisation's brand.

1. Do they already know about you or your brand or have they never heard of you?
2. Have they had a good or bad experience with you in the past?

Let's return to our graphic design agency example from the last chapter.

Here is what an ideal client profile for a graphic design agency might look like.

> The ideal client for your graphic design agency could be a startup financial service organisation based in London.
>
> The *key decision maker* working at this business is aged between 25 and 45, and could be of any gender identity. Their job title revolves around creative direction, marketing or branding, such as Head of Marketing.
>
> This key decision maker values design as an important aspect of creating a strong brand identity. They like to buy

quality products and services that represent value for money, and read industry-focused blogs and magazines.

They are likely to be active on social media, where they follow other businesses and influencers in their industry. They are not particularly interested in socialising on social media, preferring to use it for professional networking and keeping up with industry news. They tend to share posts from other brands and industry experts.

They may have heard of your business on social media, and are open to working with you. They expect a high level of professionalism and attention to detail. They have the necessary budget allocated to outsourced design services, allowing them to invest in your design work.

Here's a second example of an ideal client profile, this time for a London-based software development company.

The ideal client for your software development company is likely to be a mid-sized enterprise based in London or surrounding areas.

The key decision makers in this company are aged between 35 and 55 and could be of any gender identity. Their job title revolves around the technical side of their business, such as Chief Information Officer (CIO) or IT Manager. They are likely to have families and reside in upscale neighbourhoods within London or the suburbs.

They value innovative technology solutions that can streamline and improve their business processes, such as automation or AI. They like to buy quality products and services that represent value for money, and read tech-focused blogs and publications to stay up to date with emerging trends.

They frequent industry events and conferences, where they network with other people in their industry. They are active on social media, particularly business and employment-focused platforms, where they follow other businesses and thought leaders in their field. They use social media for work, to promote their business and engage with clients and partners.

They have already heard of your company, either through industry events or word of mouth. They expect a high level of technical expertise and professionalism from their suppliers, and are willing to invest in bespoke solutions that meet their specific needs. They have a budget allocated to outsourcing, and the authority to make purchasing decisions on behalf of their company.

Finally, here's a third example, this time for a Manchester-based fashion wholesaler.

The ideal client for your fashion wholesaler is likely to be an established fashion retailer based in Manchester. The key decision makers in this company are likely to be aged between 25 and 50, and could be of any gender identity. Their job title might be Head of Buying or an equivalent.

They may or may not have families, and are likely to reside in trendy, urban areas of Manchester.

They value trendy, affordable clothing that will appeal to their target market, as well as exceptional customer service that can help them navigate the latest fashion trends. They like to buy a wide range of products that cater to different customer segments, and read fashion-focused magazines and blogs to stay up to date with emerging fashion trends.

They tend to attend fashion shows and events, where they network with other fashion retailers and industry insiders. They are active on social media, particularly image and video-based platforms, where they follow other fashion retailers and influencers in the fashion industry. They use social media for both work and leisure, to showcase their latest collections and to engage with their customers.

They may have already heard of your company through referrals or recommendations from other fashion retailers. They expect a high level of quality and reliability from your company, and are willing to pay a competitive price for on-trend, affordable clothing that will appeal to their target market. They have a budget and the authority to make purchasing decisions on behalf of their business.

In all of these examples, there's a fair amount of guesswork.

That's okay. No storyteller has an *exact* idea of their audience, but like with your stories themselves, there are ways to learn more about what's working and what isn't to fine-tune things.

These profiles are a starting point, and you'll keep updating your ICPs as you learn more and more about your clients.

Once you have developed an ideal client profile, you need to find out what makes those key decision makers tick.

In an ideal world, you just ask them. If you have a group of clients that you can reach out to so you can ask questions about their likes and dislikes, you're onto a winner.

If you don't have the time or resources to do that, you are going to have to make do. Use your client profile to put yourself in the shoes of your ideal audience member and try to think about what motivates them. Like storytelling itself, you'll get better at this with experience.

You are going to have to make some general assumptions here, but don't let that hold you back. This is just the beginning. As you continue to develop your social media strategy, you will learn more about your audience and can finetune your ideal client profile.

Make sure to revisit your assumptions regularly. If you realise that one assumption was wrong, adjust course, and elaborate on new findings as you discover more about your clients.

Your ideal clients aren't your only audience.

Look back at your goals. You probably don't *just* want to gain new clients. You probably also want to be known within your industry, for example. In this case, you would need to appeal to experts and professional opinion formers.

Make a list of your different audiences and how they relate to your different goals.

Then, use the method we have covered in this chapter to create profiles of that audience, and arrange them in order of importance.

Once you know who your audiences are, you need to know which channels to reach them through.

You know what you want to achieve and who you want to target. You have the "who" and now you need to know the "how."

To target each of your audiences, you need to understand where they are in their buyer journey.

Broadly speaking, your future client is going to be in one of these four stages of their buyer journey: *See, Think, Do, Trust.*

Let's explore these in detail.

- **See**

    Those in the *See* stage are interested in your industry or topic. You might refer to this group as 'strangers'. They have not yet come across your brand or your social media accounts, but have an interest in the kind of content your industry features. They have no *intention* of buying or signing up to anything at this point. They are likely using social media for an unrelated reason, but are happy to read posts related to your topic. Our job as marketers is to bring awareness to strangers.

- **Think**

    Those in this stage have identified that they might need something. These are 'prospects'. They know they have a problem or challenge, and have an idea of what they want to achieve, but haven't yet made their mind up about what is going to work for them. They are doing some research into different angles and solutions. Based on an experience, an interaction or simply through awareness of us in the *See* stage, we are part of their shortlist for consideration.

- **Do**

    Those in this group have done their research on the topic and are now in a position to take action, effectively becoming 'leads'. They are ready to buy, register or sign on the dotted line. Our marketing and communication needs to easily and seamlessly allow them to take a positive action with us.

- **Trust**

    Once they become a client, it's time to both deliver on your promise (providing an exceptional service), while nurturing them and retaining their business for the years to come. Trust creates 'advocates' and advocates are happy to rebuy and refer new clients to us. Social media plays a pivotal role in the Trust stage, allowing us to maintain great relationships, and provides tools through which clients' networks can be leveraged and referrals can be easily made.

Each stage of the journey requires a different approach.

It's often assumed that social media doesn't play a huge role in *Think* and *Do* stages. In fact, for some industries, social media is the only channel that ties all of the stages together.

Take major e-commerce brands, for example. They use paid social media ads to build an audience (effectively displaying ads to those who aren't yet following them, encouraging them to engage and follow), recurring organic social media posts to stay front-and-centre of their audience's minds, and social commerce technology to sell.

Social commerce is the use of social media platforms to market and sell products and services, allowing customers complete purchases without leaving social media apps. They then ask their customer to share their experience or write a review, effectively leveraging their customers' networks.

However, it is true that social media channels often only lend themselves to the early stages of the buyer journey, especially non-paid activity. The later stages are often much more likely to be covered by search engines, Google ads, social advertising and email marketing.

Let's imagine once more that you run a graphic design agency. For now, you are concentrating on the early stages of the buyer journey.

- You build awareness of your graphic design business with those that are interested in the topic of branding: *See*
- You offer them actionable advice and valuable information that builds their trust in you as an authority on branding, especially written for those thinking about redesigning their brand or website: *Think*
- At the action stage of the journey when they have a buying intent, you then use specifically targeted Google ads focusing on cost effective logo and branding services, paired with a sales focused website, to convert those prospects into clients: *Do*
- For your existing clients, you post images of completed branding projects and graphic design tips on social media. You encourage your clients to reach out to you in your comments and private messages with questions about their graphic design. You also ask them to leave you reviews on social media: *Trust*

Which of the four stages can be covered by your social media activity? Do you have a plan for the stages that can't?

Here are some more examples of See, Think, Do, and Trust-focused activities across different sectors.

1. **Software company:**

See
Creating informative blog posts and social media content about industry trends and software development.

Think
Offering free software demos, webinars, and whitepapers that help prospects understand how the software can solve their specific problems.

Do
Providing personalised consultations and demonstrations to help prospects make a purchase decision.

Trust
Providing ongoing customer support, training, and upgrades to ensure customer satisfaction and loyalty.

2. Recruitment agency:

See
Publishing informative blog posts, social media content, and thought leadership pieces on industry topics like the state of the market and what prospective employees are looking for in their employer.

Think
Offering free consultations to help prospects identify their recruitment needs and potential strategies.

Do

Making an enquiry to discuss the specifics of running a recruitment campaign.

Trust

Maintaining regular communication with clients to provide ongoing HR advice, employee retention ideas, and infographics detailing the best time to hire new team members.

3. Management Consulting firm:

See
Creating informative blog posts and social media content about industry trends and business strategy.

Think
Offering free consultations and assessments to help prospects identify their business challenges and potential solutions.

Do
Making an enquiry to develop a customised consulting plan.

Trust
Providing ongoing support and advice to clients through regular check-ins and updates, and building long-term relationships based on trust and results.

4. Sustainable construction company:

See
Publishing informative blog posts and social media content about sustainability trends in the industry and project updates.

Think
Offering free consultations and sustainability assessments to help prospects understand their project needs and potential solutions.

Do

Making an enquiry about delivering a plan for their sustainable construction project.

Trust

Providing ongoing maintenance and support services to ensure the longevity and sustainability of completed projects, and publishing and broadcasting trends in sustainable construction.

5. **Financial Services Firm:**

See

Creating informative blog posts and social media content about financial planning, investing, and industry trends.

Think

Offering free financial assessments and consultations to help prospects understand their financial needs and potential solutions.

Do

Making an enquiry about providing a plan to help them achieve their financial goals.

Trust

Maintaining regular communication with clients through personalised advice, portfolio reviews, and performance reports. Creating and publishing content on money management, financial opinion pieces, and infographics that look back on high performing financial assets.

Look back at your audience groups and your goals. Which stage of See, Think, Do Trust does each one fit into?

If you can't tie your social media activity to reasonable and realistic SMART goals, then think again. Maybe social media is not the answer at this stage.

Look at the channels you are currently considering using and ask yourself the following questions:

1. Does my ideal audience member use this channel or are they elsewhere?
2. How do they use it? How often are they on the platform? Do they engage with and share posts? Are they a part of any groups? Do they use or engage with one particular feature or format more than others?
3. Where in the buyer journey - See, Think, Do, Trust - will they be? Do they need your service but don't know about it yet? Are they currently investigating their options? Are they already in the process of becoming a client? Are they already a client you are fostering a relationship with?
4. Does this channel help me meet my goal? If so, which goal, and how? Remember to keep it measurable.
5. What types of content are popular in this niche? Long form or short form? Are images and videos standard? Is there a focus on a particular theme, such as social issues?
6. What content pillars (the group of topics you will consistently discuss) can I create my content around?

7. How does my social activity on this channel tie into my overall strategy?

The social media world is always changing. However, if you stay attuned to your audience, their behaviour, and where they fit in the buyer journey, you will be able to pick the right channel to reach them and start telling the kind of stories that your audience is most likely to engage with

You have your SMART goals and you've identified your audience.

But how do you tell the stories they will want to share?

Key takeaways

- You can't meet your goals if you aren't targeting the right audience on the right channel.
- To understand your audience groups, you need to build profiles of your ideal audience members by answering questions about them.
- You will need to understand how these different audience groups relate to your goals and where they fit into the buyer journey (*See, Think, Do Trust*).

Original, valuable, shareable content

"Your value will not be what you know, it will be what you share."

— Ginni Rometty, former CEO of IBM

The first and last chapters of Charles Dickens' debut novel were released nineteen months apart.

In fact, he published all of his stories this way. It helped make Dickens the most successful author of his day. Why?

A complete novel was too expensive for most Victorian readers, so stories were published monthly in affordable magazines. When people were done with each issue, they could share it with someone else. Those people would then buy the next issue themselves.

Dickens' serial storytelling became the viral sensation of his day. He wasn't just writing great stories. He was writing stories designed to be easily shared using the technology of the day.

His success was thanks to a principle that we first mentioned back in Part 1.

High quality content is original, valuable and shareable.

The end goal is to find this kind of content, and then tell stories about it on social media in a way that will win you more work.

Let's break this down with another example to help you identify the best content to build your social media stories around.

Imagine you live back in Dickens' day. You are a glamorous socialite. Your friend Nancy is a baker.

Nancy bakes delicious sponge cakes made with the finest ingredients from all over the world. You're one of her regular customers. Every week, you make a visit to Nancy's Bakery to buy one of her cakes.

Like any great socialite, you love throwing dinner parties. Each of these parties has a range of attendees from different walks of life. Nancy's sponge cakes will often make an appearance for dessert. Your guests sometimes quiz you on the cake, complimenting your choice and asking where you bought it.

"It's on the high street," you say. "It's called Nancy's Bakery."

Nancy will see an influx of new customers after one of your dinner parties, and will know that you have been talking about her cakes again. As new customers come in, they each take cakes back to their families and friends.

Their families and friends ask the same question about the cakes that your guests did. Over time, Nancy's cakes become the talk of the town.

Two things are required for Nancy to keep selling more cakes.

1. The endorsement by one friend to another.
2. The quality of Nancy's sponge cakes.

People share their experience of enjoying Nancy's cakes with each other - the texture, the taste and so on. These stories become recommendations that pass from one person to the next, with customers referring their friends back to Nancy's Bakery. The quality of her cakes encourages her customers to buy more and refer their friends more often.

If you want people to share your social media content, it needs to be like Nancy's sponge cake.

- You can only get Nancy's cake in certain places - it's **original**.

- And it's delicious - it's **valuable**.

- You want to tell the world about it - it's **shareable**.

Fast forward to the present day, and we still can't resist talking to our friends about the things we love. It's not just cakes. It's information on services we use every day. It's articles on hobbies and interests. It's a news item we found online. Very often, we do all this sharing using social media.

Many organisations fall into the trap of believing that the first step in establishing their social media presence is finding lots of content to talk about. It's far more important, however, to make sure that the content you are posting is original, valuable, shareable content. How much you post depends on your organisation.

Take a news outlet, for example. They might post well over 100 times in a single day. There's news coming in all the time from all over the world. They'll be posting about everything from the latest advancements in technology to international conflicts to celebrity weddings.

On the other hand, a law firm may post around 10 times in a week. These posts might include a client review, cases they've won, legal updates, and a link to a news article. A social media post about any of these can be turned into a story.

Let's explore what it means for content to be "original, valuable and shareable" by looking at each part in turn.

Let's start with a tricky one:

High quality content is original.

You want your content to be truly original - one of a kind, a totally unique invention. But originality can be hard to define.

Ask yourself these questions:

1. **Has this been said before?**

   Your content could be an opinion based on your research in your sector or a recent industry finding, big or small. It could be a comment on an event - a statement that reflects your feelings. It needs to be something that your readers haven't heard before, anywhere else. It's personal.

2. **Have I made this post unique enough?**

   Reposting and sharing others' posts can be counterintuitively original if you add your own take, but you won't win any social media awards by playing messenger. Consider putting a similar post together using the same source, but one that reflects a different or unique viewpoint or insight. News articles from mainstream publishers or trade magazines can easily be posted with your own views attached.

3. **Is this content original in a new context?**

If you know one of your previous posts has been successful, it's perfectly fine to repost it. Just take a different angle or place it in the context of recent events.

Originality is important, but it's equally important to understand that in the sharing world of social media, originality doesn't mean creating something from scratch. It means adding insights or commentary which cannot be found elsewhere. Those insights are original to *you* or your organisation, and the stories you will tell to frame those insights and make them digestible and believable will be original to you as well

Next up:

High quality content is valuable.

You want to create something valuable - it has to have worth to your audience. Originality is one thing, but it's easy to say something no one has said before when you aren't worried about the *value* of what you're saying.

Imagine you work at a recruitment agency, for example. If a new trend emerges in your sector (like people being less likely to accept jobs that don't include working from home) you share an article on the topic with an original insight. This insight could be a story of how some of your clients are embracing hybrid working, and the staff retention benefits that are a result of that.

When people find your post valuable, it increases your credibility. This gives others a reason to follow you or engage with your posts.

It's hard to measure value, but once again there are questions you can ask that will help guide you in the right direction:

1. Is your commentary humorous? It could be topical, trivial or just plain funny.

2. Is it fact-based? Are you adding value by including statistics that contextualise a recent event, for example, and back up your original commentary.

3. Is it informative? Are you including updates on news that's relevant to your audience? To be informative, this news needs to be up to date.

4. Does it ask questions? Questions posed to your followers can get them thinking and engaged with you and your social media account. You're adding value by inviting discussion.

5. Is it insightful? Value can also come from your personal take on a situation, especially as your audience grows and you've already gained their trust.

And last but not least:

High quality content is shareable.

Shareable - is there something in your post that makes people want to share it with others? Shareability defines the perfect social media post - there's no point posting original, valuable content if it won't help to amplify your message.

When people share your social media posts, particularly in the corporate world, they are staking part of *their* trustworthiness and credibility on *your* trustworthiness and credibility. When your post is shared by others, it's an endorsement of its originality and value.

Before publishing your next social media post, ask yourself this question: would I share this content with my readers if someone else posted it? We're often our own harshest critics, so if you've answered yes, you're probably in a good spot.

Shareability is about the interaction between quality and technology. Dickens' success relied on the quality of his storytelling and the technology which allowed the cheap production of his serialised stories. The quality made people want to share his stories with others, the technology allowed them to do it.

The quality of your work will be a combination of its originality and value - that's what will get people to *want* to share it. The technology which will allow them to do so is social media, but if you haven't figured that out yet it might be worth re-reading Part 1 of this book.

Now that we've covered each part of a good post, it's important to understand that originality, value and shareability aren't independent from each other.

Originality, value and shareability all work together.

Often, if a post is original, that also makes it valuable. When it's valuable and original, it's often shareable. From another perspective, to be shareable, a post should offer value and it should be something people have never seen before.

Here are 5 more examples of original, valuable and shareable content different businesses could create.

1. **A management consultancy creating a guide on optimising productivity in the workplace.**

   This guide could be original and valuable by including unique insights and best practices for improving productivity, backed up by data and research. It could also be shareable by providing actionable tips and strategies that readers can implement in their own workplaces, as well as being designed in an eye-catching and easy-to-digest format.

2. **A manufacturing company creating a video series showcasing their production process.**

   This video series could be original and valuable by providing an inside look at the production process and highlighting the company's commitment to quality and efficiency. It could also be shareable by providing a behind-the-scenes perspective that's interesting and engaging for a wide audience, and by showcasing the products being manufactured in a visually appealing way.

3. A financial services company creating an ebook on the future of banking.

This e-book could be original and valuable by providing insights and predictions on the direction of the banking industry, backed up by expert analysis and research. It could also be shareable by providing insights that are relevant to both consumers and industry professionals, as well as being designed in a visually appealing and easily digestible format.

4. A software company creating a podcast series featuring industry thought leaders.

This podcast series could be original and valuable by featuring conversations with leading experts in the field, providing insights and perspectives that are not commonly available elsewhere. It could also be shareable by providing interesting and engaging content that's relevant to industry professionals and enthusiasts alike, as well as being promoted through social media channels and other marketing efforts.

5. A logistics company creating a blog on supply chain optimization.

This blog could be original and valuable by providing in-depth analysis and best practices for optimising the supply chain, as well as exploring emerging trends and technologies in the industry. It could also be shareable by providing practical advice and tips that are relevant to businesses of all sizes, as well as being promoted through social media.

Remember, you find the right content, and *then* you tell stories to make it believable, connect with your audience and gain their trust. Original, valuable, shareable content is the foundation - you will be telling stories *using* that content. There are plenty of opportunities for you to tell great stories within a guide, a video series, an ebook, a podcast, or a blogpost.

You know what makes high quality content.

Now, you need to use the power of storytelling to make your high quality content connect with your audience.

Key takeaways

- High quality content needs to be original, valuable and shareable.
- Originality could mean creating something entirely new, or adding a new insight to something that already exists.
- Value could mean adding humour, facts and information, asking questions or adding insights.
- Shareability means creating content which others will see value in sharing with their own followers on social media.

How to tell stories

"There's always a story. It's all stories, really. The sun coming up every day is a story. Everything's got a story in it."

— Terry Pratchett, author

Two fish are swimming in the sea.

"Water's warm today," says one. The other looks confused.

"What's water?"

It can be hard to notice something when you're surrounded by it.

However simple, you are surrounded by stories.

It's not just movies, TV shows and books. Politics, advertising, gossip, jokes, the news. Humans are constantly creating narratives to make sense of the world around us.

Learn how to spot an opportunity to turn your original, valuable and shareable content into a *story*, and you'll supercharge your content, build trust with your audience and meet your marketing goals.

In Part 1, we discussed the power of storytelling and why it works. You learned how humanity has been telling stories for thousands of years, why stories connect people on a social and psychological level and how the right story can drive an audience to take action.

This chapter will equip you with the tools to turn your content into stories.

You only need to tell simple stories to engage your audience and make your point. Although spotting opportunities to tell stories takes practice, anyone can get started with the right techniques.

So you're looking for stories to tell. But where can you find them?

Most stories you use will come from one of two places.

There are:

1. Internal stories
2. External stories

Internal stories
These come directly from your organisation or your clients. They narrativise the people and situations that your company is involved with.

External stories
These aren't about your organisation directly. Instead, you're boiling down your key message, and then telling a story that succinctly makes the same point.

Let's look at two examples.

Here is an example of an internal story.

Imagine you work for a retail franchise called MacDougal's.

Your **business goal** is to recruit more franchisees to expand the business.

Your **marketing goal** is to promote the company's culture to attract those potential franchisees.

You have reached out to several existing franchisees, hoping to find material for good stories.

One of these franchisees is named Helen. Helen first joined the company as a retail assistant when she was a teenager. In fact, it was her first job. After working at the company for fifteen years, Helen was offered the opportunity to run her own site as a franchisee. Later on, Helen took over another two sites.

Here's how you could use Helen's story to motivate prospects to consider opening a franchise, on a social media post:

> *Helen first stepped foot in a MacDougal's looking for her first job. Fifteen years later, she owns three of our sites and employs over 50 people.*
>
> *Looking to run your own business with MacDougal's? Apply on our website today.*

It might be short, but pair that with a picture of Helen beaming in front of one of her sites and you'll have turned a simple piece of information into a story about success and the enticing opportunities MacDougal's offers.

This story could also be used to supercharge a different piece of content. For example, MacDougal's social media account might share an article about a recent downtrend in social mobility.

Somebody at the company could add their own original, valuable insight, explaining that these kinds of trends are why MacDougal's has always prided itself on having so many franchisees who started as employees. That's an original, valuable, shareable bit of content, but add a story like Helen's to that and you've got something far more convincing and emotionally resonant - you've supercharged your content with storytelling.

Here's another example:

Imagine you work for a Scotland-based cleaning company named Sweep Dreams which, last year, became employee-owned.

Your **business goal** is to hire more cleaning staff.

Your **marketing goal** is to promote the company's employee ownership to encourage more people to apply to vacancies.

Not only do the employees now own the majority of shares, but an employee council has also been established to represent their voices. You talk to one of the younger employees, Maya, who has become a member of the employee council.

Recently, the council voted to support Scottish Cancer Support, a charity. While speaking to Maya, you jotted down a few quotes.

Here's how you could announce the new charity partnership while bringing Maya's story to the forefront and helping you meet your goals:

> *"Employee-ownership doesn't just help people inside our business - it helps us have an impact on everyone. I'm so*

glad we recently voted to help people in the communities we work in."

Maya joined the Sweep Dreams team three years ago. When we became employee-owned, she joined our employee council. Along with her fellow councilmembers, she is excited to announce our new charity partner: London Cancer Support.

Pair that with a picture of Maya and the employee council - or, better yet, Maya directly involved in charity work - and you've got yourself another simple but effective story. The announcement of the partnership was your original, valuable, shareable content - once again, the story works to make that content engaging, believable and emotionally resonant.

Internal storytelling is about narrativising the information you already have. That can be easier said than done. If you get stuck, here are three tips you can use to get started:

1. **Put people front and centre.**
   Every story needs characters. Your audience will be more invested in your story if they have a person to be invested in.
2. **Open with something surprising.**
   In our first example, Helen went from his first job to owning three sites. In our second example, Maya explains that employee-ownership also helps people *outside* the business, not just employees.
3. **Keep your stories concise.**
   Enough said.

To tell a story effectively, you have to draw out a character to focus on and make the stakes compelling. Then, grab your audience's attention by subverting their expectations. Like in the stories above, this is possible in just a couple of lines.

If you're able to do that, you'll be off to a great start. These are tricks storytellers have used for thousands of years. To bring back Charles Dickens from the last chapter, look at the opening line to *A Christmas Carol* - "Marley was dead: to begin with." A character is established (Marley) and an expectation is subverted (that the dead stay dead), all in just six words.

Think of how important a first line like that is to keep you reading. Think of how many stories from mythology make characters out of animals, natural phenomena like storms, and even concepts like love.

But what if you have an important point to make, but you can't find a story from inside your company? That's where external stories come in.

Here's an example of an external story.

Imagine you work for a management consulting firm.

Your **business goal** is to gain more clients.

Your **marketing goal** is to promote your team's expertise.

To do this, you're aiming to make your CEO a respected thought leader using social media.

Here's a story your CEO could tell on social media to help meet that goal:

> *The French military commander and political leader Napoleon Bonaparte faced one of his greatest triumphs and one of his greatest failures just a month apart.*
>
> *He was a famous micromanager. This worked well on land, where he could send messages to his men with ease. His eye for detail helped the French win an overwhelming victory at the Battle of Austerlitz.*
>
> *The Battle of Trafalgar, however, was fought at sea. There, distant ship captains needed to be able to make their own split-second decisions. The French suffered a crushing defeat.*
>
> *To overcome challenges in any terrain, you need to know when to take control and when to empower your team...*

The character of Napoleon is set up and an expectation is subverted right away. The subverted expectation is that Napoleon's greatest success and failure were probably on the opposite ends of his career. Then, the story continues by unravelling the lesson behind that subverted expectation - that you need to empower your team to be flexible and succeed - so that it's relevant to the audience.

Here's another example.

Imagine you work for a marketing agency called ABC Limited, with many clients in the tech sector.

As with the previous story, your **business goal** is to gain more clients and your **marketing goal** is to promote your team's expertise. Here's a story a team member could tell to do just that:

> *In the 1970s, computer scientist Grace Hopper was working on a new programming language that would be easier for ordinary people to use.*
>
> *At the time, most programming languages used complex mathematical notation. In contrast, Hopper's new language used plain English words and phrases to describe programming concepts, such as "IF...THEN...ELSE" statements.*
>
> *Hopper's innovations weren't always welcomed by her male colleagues, who saw her language as "dumbing down" programming. In response, Hopper famously said, "I'm not trying to make the language more complex, I'm trying to make it more accessible."*
>
> *Innovation isn't about making things more complicated. It's about making things simpler. That's why at ABC Limited, we're dedicated to making your message easy to understand.*

This story doesn't subvert an expectation right away - you don't have to be that formulaic - but it does set up a character, and then relate the lesson from the story to its audience's wants.

You'll find stories just like these throughout this book. Like internal stories, external stories often start with a focus on one character, and kick off with a surprising twist.

However, as our second example shows, you don't have to follow this formula - these are just techniques to help you get started. You can tell stories in many different ways to meet many different goals.

External stories aren't directly about your organisation. Instead, they are an opportunity to introduce storytelling from outside your organisation to make a point that's relevant to your audience. In this case, that point is the importance of delegating.

There are plenty of situations where you can use an exterior story to demonstrate your point, but be careful. It's sometimes easy to get carried away with a story, without realising that it doesn't quite make the point you want it to.

Your story needs to contain your key message.

Take a look at this alternate introduction to a chapter from Part 1 of this book, titled *Social Animals*. This story was originally written for that chapter to demonstrate the power of storytelling, but it was cut and replaced. See if you can figure out why:

> *Mike was on the cusp of a breakthrough which would kickstart his meteoric rise from underdog to alpha male. All it would take was two cans of kerosene.*
>
> *Mike was a chimpanzee under Jane Goodall's observation at the Gombe Stream Research Centre in the 1960s. He was at the bottom of the pecking order, bullied by the other chimps.*

In her book In the Shadow of Man, *Goodall recalls the day that Mike's social status changed for good. Having collected two kerosene cans from the nearby research camp, he approached the other males and their leader, Goliath. Slowly, Mike began banging the cans together. The din grew into a cacophony. Then, he charged. Terrified, the other chimps scattered. None of them gave Mike trouble after that.*

Using tools isn't unique to humans. It's been observed across the animal kingdom, from crows to octopuses. Complex social structures and rich emotional lives aren't unique either.

But before Jane Goodall, the social lives of chimps were a mystery. Her work didn't just deliver insights into their world. It transformed them in the popular consciousness from animals into underdogs, heroes, even warring tribes. It was a revolution in primatology, but also storytelling. Without Goodall's work, Mike and his kerosene cans would be long forgotten. So what is it that sets us apart from our closest cousins?

Humans have evolved an impulse to share stories.

In your marketing, stories are one of your most powerful tools.

It's an interesting story, but does it actually make the point we're trying to make? Boiled down, the opening point of the *Social Animals* chapter is this:

> Stories build trust. Trust builds social networks.

Mike's story is compelling and it could be used to make plenty of points:

- Humans aren't the only ones who use tools.
- Brains can be better than brawn.
- Being an outcast can force you to think outside the box.

However, Mike's story doesn't make the chapter's point nearly as clearly as the story we ended up using about the Agta people, who straight-forwardly use stories to build trust and social networks in their society.

Your story has to serve your message. Your message cannot be retrofitted to serve a good story. That's how you lose sight of your goals

To tell the right story, you need to understand your key message.

That means boiling down your main point to just one or two short sentences. You can do this by looking back at your goals.

For example, imagine that your organisation is a management consultancy, and your goal is to get more clients. Your main point, then, might be "an outsider perspective can find solutions that an insider cannot."

Then, you need to boil down the point of any story you're considering telling to its core lesson. In our example, you need to find a story about an outsider's fresh perspective allowing them to solve a solution that insiders couldn't see.

If the lesson of your story doesn't match your main point one for one, you'll need to find a different story or figure out a different way to tell it. Otherwise, your story isn't going to help you meet your goal.

The fact that the story about Mike the chimpanzee needs several paragraphs to link it to the chapter's main point is evidence that it might not be the right fit. If you can't tell your story succinctly and easily link it to your message, it might not be the right choice.

Your stories don't need to be non-fiction and they don't need to be long. Take a look at the story that starts this chapter:

> *Two fish are swimming in the sea.*
>
> *"Water's warm today," says one. The other looks confused.*
>
> *"What's water?"*
>
> *It can be hard to see something when you're surrounded by it.*
>
> *You are surrounded by stories.*

This is just an old joke, but it sets a scene, it gives us characters and it has a fun twist. It's everything we need to cut to the chase and dive right into this chapter.

Here are some other places you can draw inspiration, with example stories for each.

You can use personal experience.

I can't stand sweetcorn.

It's not sweetcorn's fault. There's just something about it. Even when it's buried under a mountain of other flavours, just knowing it's hiding in there is enough to make my stomach turn.

A lot of people have that one food they detest. It can border on a phobia. Matters of taste are hard to rationalise. For someone else, that food you can't stomach could be a delicacy.

This poses a major problem for marketers: there's nothing more subjective than the act of consumption...

You can rework famous anecdotes.

It was the height of the space race, and NASA had a problem.

Pens don't work in zero gravity. A brief panic and several thousands of dollars of R&D later, and voila! NASA had invented a pen that worked in space.

The Russians used a pencil.

So maybe that story's apocryphal, but there's a reason it caught on.

Sometimes, we get so bogged down trying to get our approach to work that we can't see a simple solution...

You can use stories from other industries.

In April 2012, the video game company Electronic Arts won the "Worst Company in America" award with over 50,000 votes.

EA spokesperson John Reseburg was having none of it:

"We're sure that bank presidents, oil, tobacco and weapons companies are all relieved they weren't on the list this year. We're going to continue making award-winning games and services played by more than 300 million people worldwide."

The next year, EA won the award again.

When your customers are telling you something, listen...

You can use stories about famous figures.

On the day of his death, doctors had drained George Washington of almost half of his blood. They were attempting to cure a throat infection.

It's easy for us to look back on the medical practices of the past with disbelief, but in some cases bloodletting can help

> people. Even today, you can take a turn off the motorway just ten miles out from Swansea and find Biopharm Leeches, the NHS's official leech provider.
>
> By drawing blood, leeches prevent blood from coagulating and speed up the healing process. This might lead to an incorrect assumption - draining blood helps a patient heal.
>
> Sometimes, someone having a small amount of knowledge is worse than knowing nothing at all. We always risk turning one correct observation (like bloodletting speeding up the healing process) into an incorrect assumption (that draining half of someone's blood will heal them even quicker)...

These are examples to get you started.

Some of these stories can also be reworked from different angles to make different points.

Here's how you could repurpose the last story to make a new point.

> Take a turn off the motorway just outside Swansea and you'll find Biopharm Leeches, the NHS's official leech provider.
>
> Most of us think of medical leeches as a thing of the past. The truth is, they still work wonders. Leeches prevent blood from coagulating and speed up the healing process.

As the old saying goes, if it ain't broke, don't fix it. That's true in our industry as well…

You can find useful stories from across all aspects of life.

Even if you're writing stories about events in and around your organisation, you can still apply some of the same techniques these stories use to make them more enticing.

However, although there will be plenty of stories you can tell that come from within your organisation and from your clients, keep this quote from marketing consultant and New York Times bestseller Jay Baer in mind:

"If your stories are all about your products and services, that's not storytelling. It's a brochure. Give yourself permission to make the story bigger."

Remember the story from Part 1 that Steve Jobs told when announcing the Apple Macintosh?

"IBM wants it all and is aiming its guns to its last obstacle to industry control. Apple. Will Big Blue dominate the entire computer industry?"

This is a perfect example of making the story bigger. It tells a story about giants and underdogs, freedom and control, monopoly versus innovation.

You have some of the simple storytelling tools to get you started, but never let storytelling become a box ticking exercise.

Mediocre speeches begin "I'd like to start by telling a story." Great speeches have a story infused throughout that delivers their point with an emotional punch.

Remember that storytelling taps into a fundamental part of the human psyche. It's how we've made friends, given warnings, created coherent social groups, and understood the world around us for thousands of years.

We see our world in stories. Our perception is always limited, always narrativised, and always infused with emotion.

Never limit the ambition of your storytelling. Storytelling brought Apple back from the brink of disaster, it allowed the Agta to survive as one of the few hunter-gatherer societies left on the planet. Storytelling, a grand narrative about good and evil, freedom and tyranny, put man on the moon.

You'll need original, valuable and shareable content, but your competitors will have that too.

To come out on top, you need to tell the better story.

Key takeaways

- There are stories everywhere.
- Sometimes you will tell internal stories - stories that are about your business, your clients and the people involved in both.

- Other times, you will tell external stories - stories which make the same point that you are trying to make as an analogy.
- Stories can be sourced from practically anywhere from history to first-hand experience.
- The more your practice recognising and telling stories, the more powerful your content will become.

Attracting your audience and maintaining relationships

"You can make more friends in two months by becoming interested in other people than you can in two years by trying to get other people interested in you."

— Dale Carnegie, *How to Win Friends and Influence People*

Jay-Z has sold over 27 million albums. In the mid-'90s, he couldn't get a record deal.

He had an original sound, he had something to say, he even had finished tracks. What he didn't have was an audience.

He didn't wait for an audience to come to him. He went straight to his target audience and engaged with them directly. In 1995, along with Damon Dash and Kareem Burke, he parked in the streets of New York City and sold CDs out of his car. This gave them the chance to talk to people about their newly formed, independent record label: Roc-A-Fella Records.

This grassroots approach helped Jay-Z build a loyal fanbase in New York. He was talking to people, so people started talking about him.

With Jay-Z as its figurehead, Roc-A-Fella became one of the most influential record labels of all time.

Don't wait for your audience to come to you. You need to seek out and engage with your audience directly.

You've already learned where social media fits into the buyer journey, how important it is to understand your audience and how the power of storytelling can supercharge your original, valuable, shareable content.

This chapter is about attracting people to your social media and maintaining your relationship with your audience.

Your social media has two types of potential followers.

1. Those who don't know you.
2. Those who do.

You need to apply a different set of attraction techniques depending on which group you're dealing with.

For the second group (your existing contacts and clients), you'll be focusing on the big picture. This means promoting your social media activity through your existing communication channels. This could include email newsletters, your website, even business cards.

For now, let's focus on attracting people who don't know you yet.

You need to build an audience of qualified followers.

Qualified followers are people who are genuinely interested in what you're selling and the content you're posting. These are the people you need to start and maintain a relationship with.

Fortunately, there are principles of attraction that work across all platforms.

Locate your audience on a given platform.

As we discussed earlier in this book, you need to identify your audience based on your goals.

One way to find your audience on social media is by identifying your competitors or influencers within your industry (we assume here that competitors and influencers have the same ideal customer profile as you).

Almost all social media platforms will allow you to see who's following who. With that in mind, search for your industry influencers, locate their account and see who's following them. This is a powerful way to get an initial list of people who'll be interested in your organisation and its service offering.

Alternatively, search for a post that's relevant to your industry and has received a large amount of shares or views. See who's liked it, made a positive comment or other type of engagement.

Using the above ideas, you can begin to put together an initial list of people you can start following and engage with.

Engage with your audience.

Acknowledging other people's original, valuable and shareable posts will grab their attention. Getting engagement on social media releases dopamine, sometimes known as the happiness hormone[9]. The truth is a bit more complicated.

Dopamine is a neurotransmitter (a chemical messenger in the brain) that plays a crucial role in your physiology and behaviour. It belongs to a class of chemicals known as catecholamines, which also includes adrenaline.

Dopamine has several functions, but it is best known for its involvement in the brain's reward and pleasure pathways. It's the "feel-good" neurotransmitter.

Dopamine doesn't just contribute to feelings of pleasure - it's also connected to sensations of motivation and positive reinforcement.

Thanks to dopamine, a simple action like liking, sharing or commenting on another post can help start a social media relationship. It doesn't just give the person whose post you're engaging with that "feel-good" feeling. It will also motivate them to engage with you.

That's because, like the oxytocin that releases when we share stories, dopamine reinforces behavioural patterns. If your account is associated with good feelings, people are going to engage with it.

The more you genuinely engage with others on social media, the more they will engage with you.

Combine the dopamine from engagement with the oxytocin you get sharing stories and engaging with your audience on social media with a story can release a powerful chemical cocktail.

Engaging with others will pull in views to your profile and get your new posts noticed and shared. Depending on the quality of your posts, sometimes simply following others will lead to them following you back. If not, you need a more direct approach.

Start the conversation.

Be the one to approach influencers or industry experts with views and get them to engage with you. Talk to others in your industry or to your followers directly to spark a conversion.

However, it's important to make sure you don't become a nuisance. Your comments and outreach need to be valuable to your audience, just like your posts.

You can build "followers campaigns" on some platforms.

These are paid advertising campaigns designed to get you more followers. Exactly how they work will depend on the platform, but here's some good advice to get started.

Begin by putting together a list of people you want to follow you, based on a set of criteria. For example, you may want people to follow you because of the influencers they follow, their previous posts and activity, their location or language, or their interests.

Once you have identified your audience, you can begin targeting them with your followers campaign.

In theory, you can do this on many platforms by picking your best performing post - e.g. the one with the most engagements - and turning it into a paid promoted post. When you pay for a promoted post, you will almost always get the option to define the audience you want to target.

In practice, you're likely to find more success by creating a paid promoted campaign with specific goals and messaging and using it to target this audience, rather than boosting specific posts.

These are good first steps to attracting an audience.

But how do you maintain your relationship with them?

Social media gives everyone the opportunity to stay connected, keep in touch, maintain relationships and build community.

It's the perfect way to keep your clients, customers, and other contacts up to date with what you're doing, while making the conversation two way. It's easy to share a moment or two with your audience every day.

You can do that in a way that not only maintains that relationship, but enhances it and helps you meet your goals.

People use social media in many different ways.

They might connect with their boss in hopes of moving up the career ladder. They might chat with like-minded music fans. They might just share recipes for Friday night's dinner.

Each of those users have a purpose. In order to engage with them, we need to understand how they're using social media on that particular social media channel at that particular time.

Every industry changes. New developments, new products, new methods. You can keep your audience keen by researching and representing the cutting edge of your industry.

The internet is awash with articles, mostly free. Websites, trade magazines, journals and other news sources can provide you with valuable, shareable content that can be turned into a compelling story and spark a new conversation with your existing followers.

Search online for ten blogs, news sources and online trade magazines. Shortlist this down to five or six, and subscribe to their news feed. It may also be worth investing in one or two of these online journals through a paid subscription.

Not only will this provide you with high quality information, you'll also have that information before many of your competitors. This makes your social media account the first place many users in your audience will get this information. Already, you're building trust, building credibility and maintaining a great relationship with your audience.

Focus less on selling and more on teaching, coaching and engagement.

The buying process does not start with a sale, it starts with a "hello."

Know where your audience is in the buyer journey: *See, Think, Do, Trust*. This is broken down in more detail in the earlier chapter *Targeting the right audience and channel*.

Your social media content should be more about building trust in the long term, not jumping straight to the sale while failing to offer valuable content. To do that, you don't just need to tell stories, you need to give your audience a little insight into the storyteller if you're going to gain their trust.

When posting via social media, don't hide behind your logo or your brand.

No one likes talking to robots or the feeling like they're communicating with someone that doesn't understand their needs. On social media, exposure can provide a level of vulnerability that disarms your audience and potential buyers.

Look out for the telltale signs. You'll know you're hiding behind your logo if you feel more comfortable referring to "yourself" as "we" (except in the case of this book of course, where there are three of us).

Start using "I." This will make prospects and clients feel like you are taking personal responsibility for your content and your company. This is a very powerful feeling. By switching to the first person, you can build trust quicker and maintain a strong bond with your audience on an individual level. It's the perfect opportunity to tell stories - your story - from a first-person perspective.

People like people. If they feel there is a person behind a brand - a real person that they can talk to and emotionally connect with - they are much more likely to engage in a longer term social media relationship.

When you feel ready, it's time to leverage that relationship.

Now that you're building and maintaining these relationships, you can start to softly share the benefits of your services more directly and explicitly.

By telling stories around your original, valuable, shareable content you are building loyalty. You are giving users a reason to engage with your content. When this happens often enough, you reach a tipping point.

This tipping point, in business and sales terms, is the point at which a series of small events become significant enough to cause a larger, more important change.

In social media terms, these small events are the times people engage with your posts. This will eventually build your credibility to such a level that every post will be engaged with a significant number of times.

This mounting credibility will see you get more followers, even more engagement and, eventually, financial reward.

The more qualified followers you have, the more qualified followers you'll get.

Credibility becomes easier to acquire at this level. It takes a shorter amount of time for a potential buyer to trust you simply by the mere fact that you've received a significant amount of third-party endorsements.

There's one more piece of good practice that you can use along the way to maintain relationships with your followers.

Respond. Mention. Thank.

- **Respond**

    Respond to questions, comments, suggestions and, if appropriate, to opinions about your content. Remember that these conversations are often very public - respond in a reactive or defensive way and you'll negatively impact your reputation. This is an opportunity to show the entire social media world what kind of organisation you represent through the level of engagement you have with your followers.

- **Mention**

    Seen something someone else has done well? This is a great opportunity to engage with someone and tag them in a comment or post. They're likely to get a notification themselves of your activity, so this is another way to get your brand and your name on their radar.

- **Thank**

    A "Thank You" to a follower or social media user who has shared your content can go a long way to show that you care about their actions, and appreciate the endorsement.

Engage with your audience and they will engage with you.

Once your audience reaches a certain size, you will begin to see these users communicating amongst themselves. Remember how we ended the first chapter of this book?

What's more powerful than telling a great story that wins you more work?

Convincing others to tell your story for you.

Key takeaways

- Don't wait for your audience to come to you - go to them!
- You can attract an audience of qualified followers by exploring pre-existing communities and topics in your area of expertise on a given platform.
- Engage with the people you need to attract, creating content useful to them, not selling to them.
- When people begin engaging with your posts, respond to them, mention them and thank them.

Influencing influencers

"It's easy to get people's attention, what counts is getting their interest."

— A. Philip Randoplh, civil rights activist

After graduating from university, Sara Blakely was a door-to-door fax machine sales rep and part-time standup comedian.

Frustrated by the uncomfortable tights she had to wear for her day job, Sara set out to develop an alternative. After two years of development, that alternative became the women's apparel brand Spanx.

Naturally, she wanted to get the word out there. She managed to get funding for a broad advertising campaign. She even appeared on the Oprah Winfrey Show. But after an initial boost, sales began to slow down.

That's when Sara remembered something from her door-to-door sales days. Instead of trying to convince everyone, she decided to focus on convincing people who were already part of the way there. She decided to focus on a niche, contacting wedding planners and event coordinators to promote Spanx to women attending formal events.

It wasn't just that Sara had narrowed the scope of her marketing. She specifically targeted the people - like wedding planners - who had the ear of her audience.

Sales skyrocketed. In 2012, Forbes named Sara Blakely the youngest female self-made billionaire.

You can't try to target everyone at once. Target people who will share your content and help it reach an engaged audience that cares.

Imagine you buy the same newspaper every week (maybe you do). That single newspaper will have tens of thousands of readers. A free, daily newspaper might have hundreds of thousands of readers.

However, the newspaper isn't the content creator. It's just the channel through which the content is served. Similarly, social media is the channel through which your content will be served. Social media platforms don't generate content themselves, they serve it up.

If you wanted to hire a PR agency to help promote your service, you would approach an agency that has strong contacts with journalists that cover your field.

If you were a graphic design agency, for example, and were releasing a new design service, you would want to contact a PR agency that had good relationships with journalists in the world of graphic design and marketing. Then, the PR agency would approach the journalist with your new service and ask them to review it.

The website or magazine they write for is the channel, and gets editorial exposure for your service. It's a way for your audience to find out that your product exists.

You need to apply the exact same thinking when it comes to online PR, and PR through social media.

You have your social media channels. Now, you need to find the content providers.

This means finding journalists or influencers on social media who have a large audience in your area of expertise or service market.

To start, you need to identify those influencers.

For now, we will be using the term influencer instead of journalist. Although most journalists are influencers, not all influencers are journalists. Influencers come in all shapes and sizes, with different specialisms, interests and audiences. What they have in common is a large following.

While it is possible to pay for influencer endorsements, it isn't always recommended. Many celebrities will endorse products on social media, for example. If you want to go down that route, contact the celebrity's agent or use influencer directory platforms. However, there's often a better way.

You can influence influencers without the price tag.

Micro-influencers are influencers without major celebrity status. Instead, they have a relatively large but more niche following in a particular area.

You have probably found yourself in a situation where you have written a great piece of content and shared it on social media, only to find it hasn't got much attention. Then, you see a similar post by a key micro-influencer which has received far more exposure and engagement.

It is hard getting the same kind of exposure as a micro-influencer in your industry, even if your post quality is the same.

When micro-influencers share your stories, the exposure of your post (and potentially future posts) can be huge.

But how do you get micro-influencers to share your stories?

First, you have to figure out who is willing to share your content. Often, it's people who have already shared others' content in the past. For example, if a micro-influencer has already shared someone else's post on the *Top 10 Graphics Design Tips*, wouldn't they be willing to share another post about a new graphic design service?

Get your post in front of someone who's already shared content like it before.

You can get started by following this simple 4 step process:

1. Find influencers in your niche.
2. Analyse these influencers.
3. Build a relationship.
4. Reach out, using the power of storytelling.

Start by finding influencers in your niche.

Hashtags are a great way to find influencers in your niche, and almost all social media platforms use them. For example, if you look up the hashtag #GraphicDesign on one of the platforms you're using, you can then sort through the top and most recent popular posts.

Then, you can analyse the influencers that you find.

Browse through the content that you find in your niche, and look at the profiles of the people who are posting it. Note their audience, size, location, and the general theme of their account. You can even use analytics tools to look at their engagement rate, how often they post, and other information about their audience. Look for influencers who have large, engaged audiences that match your client profile.

Once you've found your influencers, it's time to start building a relationship.

You can do this by following and engaging with their account. This will help put you on their radar. You can continue this activity for as long as you feel comfortable, until you're ready to leverage that relationship for the next step.

Now, you can reach out.

You can approach them directly through direct messages. Many will also have an email address in their social media profile bio which you can use to contact them.

Reaching out needs to be genuine and considered.

Take the below example, and feel free to adapt and use it yourself.

Imagine you're reaching out to an influencer named Kate, a micro-influencer in the world of graphic design whose audience is largely Birmingham-based SMBs - your target audience.

You have been engaging with Kate on social media by following her account, replying to her posts and mentioning and tagging her for a few weeks. You refer to pieces of content Kate has written or shared.

For example:

> *"@Kate loved this take on graphic design. Interesting tips there. Feeling inspired. Expect an article soon!"*

Kate will very likely like your post.

Next, you research the influencer a little more by finding her blog, reviewing the articles she's written and leaving a couple of comments.

Now that Kate is aware that you and her share similar interests and have similar audiences, your next step is to write an article on a topic in both of your areas of interest. Draw her in with a story. Then, reach out to Kate via email, to tell her and ask for feedback.

> *Hi Kate,*
>
> *Remember I promised you an article on graphic design? Well, here it is. I'd really love your thoughts on it.*
>
> *Here's the article: [LINK]*

All the best,
[Your name]
[Your social media handle]

This email has a few features that make it more likely to work:

1. It's short. Around 50 words once the gaps are filled in.

2. It doesn't look like spam. A longer message may appear to be so.

3. It's personal. This isn't time for a mass email with "mail merged" information.

4. It points the micro-influencer in the direction of your article, but does not ask them to do anything with it specifically. They'll come to the conclusion that it's worth sharing for themselves. Your job here is to simply point out that this article you've written exists.

Once you've begun to reach out to these influencers, sit back and await the responses.

To give you an idea of "success rate" (this will depend on the relationship you have built up), you should be hoping that 20% respond.

Remember, you are trying to provide them with content that they can share - and be the first to do so - so that they remain the source of new information for their followers. From this perspective, you're doing them a favour by providing original and valuable content for them to share. Once you see this as a mutually beneficial relationship, you'll be encouraged to continue writing stories using original, valuable and shareable content.

After the first time a micro-influencer has shared your content, you can be sure they'll keep you in mind in the future. However, it doesn't hurt to give them a nudge every now and again. Don't forget to keep engaging and building on this relationship as you go, sharing each other's content.

Over time, as your list of influencers grows, your access to the market will grow as well.

You will begin to see an increase in your own following on the relevant social media channels. However, it's important to remember that it always comes down to providing those great stories around original, valuable, shareable content to begin with.

Here are 3 final tips on micro-influencer engagement:

1. Give your micro-influencers the feeling that they're getting the opportunity to share something first. Maybe even get them to add something to your piece or make a recommendation before you publish it, as they are likely to share it with their followers. Then it's publicity for them as well!

2. Write something specifically for their audience - a compelling story they'll engage with, perhaps with people or characters they'll be familiar with - and reach out directly to tell them what you've done. It's like doing their job for them. They'll love you for it.

3. Sing their praises. Give them shout-outs every once in a while.

Once you've targeted the right people to get your stories out there, you need to know how to measure the results.

Key takeaways

- You can't try to target everyone at once. Target people who will share your content and help it reach the right audience.
- Start by finding influencers in your niche.
- Analyse these influencers, noting their audience, size, location, and the general theme of their account.
- Engage with their account and, when you've built a relationship, reach out to them directly with the opportunity to share something you've created first.

Measuring success

"Without data, you're just another person with an opinion."

— W. Edwards Deming, engineer and statistician

In 2016, Senator Jim Inhofe brought a snowball to the hall of the United States Senate, and tossed it to the sitting senate President.

"Because we keep hearing that 2014 has been the warmest year on record," said Inhofe, "I ask the chair, you know what this is? It's a snowball just from outside here."

It's a classic refrain - if the world is warming up, why is it so cold out?

Senator Inhofe was right. There was snow outside in Washington DC on that day. The problem, however, is that personal experience only ever offers one point on the graph. A single observation by itself can be correct, while not representing the trends in the data at large.

You need data.

Without data, your perspective will be extremely limited. You won't have the details on which parts of your social media output are performing well and which are not.

When running a story-driven social media campaign, it can be very tempting to judge the stories based on taste - the way we do when watching TV, reading a book or seeing a film. Just because your output is stories, however, that doesn't mean you don't need hard data to make decisions.

Measuring and analysing your engagement statistics can help you to make informed decisions about your strategy and future posts. It can also help you find out whether all the effort you put into a given channel has had the desired effect, or if you are simply wasting your time.

So how do you measure success?

Get your goals in front of you. Remember that everything that we do on social media needs to be directly relatable to one of our goals.

Here are some metrics that you can measure and the goals that they might be related to:

- **Reach and exposure**
  Getting people to know your brand.
- **In-channel engagement**
  Creating a community and building lasting engagement.
- **Actions (off-channel engagement)**
  Getting people to perform an action, like clicking a link to your website.
- **Conversions**
  Getting people to fill out a form or contact you, and then turning those leads into clients through your current pitching or offline method.

How to measure reach and exposure:

The concept of reach and exposure applies across all social media channels.

"Reach" refers to the number of unique individuals who were shown a particular piece of content on a social media platform. It doesn't necessarily mean that they engaged with the content or clicked on it.

"Exposure" refers to the number of times a particular piece of content was displayed to a user on a social media platform, including repeat views by the same user. This metric takes into account both unique views and multiple views by the same individual.

Reach and exposure can be measured through metrics like "reach" and "impressions." The exact name depends on the channel. Most social media platforms will have their own analytics services which will allow you to see these metrics.

Remember that familiarity with your brand is a crucial factor in the people you're reaching's decision making process. However, exposure is very difficult to equate with success. So, let's look at the next set of metrics we can measure, which are a little less vague.

- **Observation**

    Your company's posts have a high reach, but a low engagement rate.

    Conclusion

    Your company may want to explore why users are not

engaging with your content, and experiment with different types of content or calls-to-action to increase engagement.

- **Observation**

    Your company's account has a high impression rate, but a low reach rate.

    Conclusion

    Your company may want to explore why your account is not reaching as many users as they would like, and experiment with different types of content or hashtags to increase reach.

Here are some examples of "reach and exposure" statistics and the conclusions you could draw from them.

1. **Observation**

    Your posts on one of your channels have a high reach, but a low engagement rate.

    Conclusion

    You may want to explore why users are not engaging with your content, and experiment with different types of content or calls-to-action to increase engagement.

2. **Observation**

    Your account on a social media platform has a high impression rate, but a low reach rate.

    Conclusion

    You may want to explore why your account is not reaching as many users as you would like, and experiment with different types of content or hashtags to increase reach.

3. **Observation**

    Your page on a social media platform has a high engagement rate, but a low reach rate.

    Conclusion

    You may want to explore why your page is not reaching as many users as you would like, and experiment with different types of content or paid advertising to increase reach.

4. Observation

Your content on one of your channels has a high reach, but a low engagement rate.

Conclusion

You may want to explore why users are not engaging with your content, and experiment with different types of content or calls-to-action to increase engagement.

5. Observation

Your videos on a video platform have a high impression rate, but a low engagement rate.

Conclusion

You may want to explore why users are not engaging with your videos, and experiment with different types of content or calls-to-action to increase engagement.

How to measure in-channel engagements:

"In-channel engagements" refer to interactions and actions that occur directly within a specific social media channel. These actions are taken by users on the channel, without navigating to external sites.

In-channel engagements include likes, comments, shares, clicks, mentions and follows, depending on the channel you're using. Broadly speaking, however, in-channel engagements can be broken down on two levels.

The first level of in-channel engagements is post engagement.

This includes metrics like likes, reactions, reposts, shares, comments, replies, mentions and tags - anything that requires action on the channel from the person looking at your post. This can also include metrics like media, video or story views and the number of times a post was expanded.

Just like reach and exposure, you'll find these stats in your channel analytics. These metrics show you how engaging your posts are and how engaged your audience is. If your audience isn't familiar with your content, you want to strive for an engagement rate beyond 1% for each post. If they are familiar with it, aim for 2-5%.

Look at your most successful posts. See whether you can find a pattern in the content or the tone that can be tied to their success. This can help you understand which of your posts are working, and on which level. Some might be great for getting more exposure (with a high amount of shares) for example, while others might work better at building your community (with more replies and comments).

The second level of in-channel engagements is profile engagements.

This includes metrics like follows. These actions actively build your audience. This means that the next time you post (or promote a post) you will have more engaged people to reach.

You'll find these stats in your channel's analytics area as before, so make sure to check them each month to see how your following is growing so that your content is reaching more and more people in your target audience.

Here are some examples of "in-channel engagement" statistics and the conclusions you could draw from them.

1. Observation

Your business' engagement rate on Platform A is consistently above 5%, while their engagement rate on Platform B is below 1%.

Conclusion

You may want to focus more on creating content that resonates with your audience on Platform A, and re-evaluate your strategy on Platform B.

2. Observation

Your stories on a video platform have high views but low engagement rates.

Conclusion

You may want to experiment with different types of content or incorporate calls-to-action, questions, or invite comments to encourage engagement.

3. Observation

Your most successful posts showcase employees and company culture.

Conclusion

You may want to prioritise creating more content that highlights your employees and culture.

4. Observation

Your account on one platform has seen a significant increase in followers over the past month.

Conclusion

You may want to analyse what you are doing differently on this platform, who those followers are (spot any micro-influencers), or particular content that did well, and incorporate it into their other social media channels.

5. Observation

Your videos have high views and engagement, but low audience retention rate.

Conclusion

You may want to explore the length or format of their content to better retain viewers.

How to measure actions:

Actions, off-channel engagement, take the user from your social media post to elsewhere. This could mean the user clicked a link in one of your posts, or viewed your website.

Like the other metrics, you can find these in each channel's analytics area. You can also verify these stats using your website analytics like Google Analytics.

Cross-referencing clicks with website views allows you to verify how many people landed on your site and what they did there. This can give you a huge amount of insight into your audience's behaviour.

Did they stick around to read your article or just abandon it within a few seconds? Did they go on to read more of your articles, or just leave after the first one? Did they browse your website or not? Are they actual people or just bots?

Here are some examples of "action" statistics and the conclusions you could draw from them.

1. **Observation**

    Your posts with links to your website have a high click-through rate, but a low website view rate.

    Conclusion

    You may want to explore why users are not staying on your website after clicking on a post, and optimise your landing pages or website content to encourage further engagement.

2. **Observation**

    Your posts with links to your blog have a high bounce rate.

Conclusion

You may want to explore why users are not staying on your blog after clicking on a post, and optimise your blog content to encourage further engagement.

3. Observation

Your posts with links to your product page have a high conversion rate.

Conclusion

You may want to prioritise creating more content that directs users to your product page, as it appears to be effective in driving conversions.

4. Observation

Your image posts with links to your website have a low click-through rate.

Conclusion: You may want to explore why users are not clicking on your links on image posts, and experiment with different types of content or calls-to-action.

5. Observation

Your videos with links to your website have a high click-through rate, but a low website view rate.

Conclusion: You may want to explore why users are not staying on your website after clicking on a video link, and potentially optimise your landing pages or website content to encourage further engagement.

How to measure conversions:

Conversions are the holy grail. They are why you're doing what you're doing. These metrics are about measuring how many of your users have actually turned into real leads or clients.

Your conversions can be things like newsletter sign ups, contact form submissions or online purchases. What you class as a conversion will count on your company and website.

Because they differ by business, to track conversions you will need to define them in your website analytics software.

When looking at the channel a conversion came from, it's important not to jump to conclusions. Just because one of the channels you're using has a lower number of conversions against it, that does not necessarily mean it isn't contributing. One channel might be great at getting people to visit your website, with those same people returning to your website at a later date and becoming clients then.

Google Analytics is a treasure trove of insight if you know how to use it. If you don't, there are other ways you can start comparing your metrics against others in your industry. Here are some simple activities you can use to get started, even if you don't have a reporting platform:

- Compare your followers and likes with those of industry experts and find a follow count goal you want to reach.

- Benchmark your post engagement against posts by others in your industry that you found very interesting.
- Take a note of an increased level of emails or calls you get and try to link these to social activity.
- Actually ask your clients how they found you and whether they read your social posts and get some real life feedback from them.

Measuring your campaign's results on social media allows you to quantify the success of something that's usually considered subjective: the success of your storytelling.

By measuring key metrics and analysing data, you can gain valuable insights and make informed decisions. This allows you to do one of the most important things in social media marketing.

Continually measure and optimise your social media strategy.

Key takeaways

- Measurement is crucial for understanding social media performance and making informed decisions.
- In-channel engagement metrics (e.g. likes, shares, comments) show how engaging your posts are and audience engagement levels.
- Profile engagements (e.g. follows) actively build your audience and expand reach.
- Action metrics track off-channel engagements like clicks, website views, and conversions.

- Analysing all of these metrics helps identify areas for improvement and experiment with different content types or strategies.

PART 3

Telling your stories on social media

"A picture is worth a thousand words."

— Anon

You know the power of storytelling. You've built your social media strategy. But what does the finished product actually look like? It's time to put it all together.

Part 3 of this book is packed full of examples to show how you can harness the power of storytelling. Each part's title refers to the type of content the example stories are being told around, to help you get to grasps with telling stories with a wide variety of content to meet an equally wide variety of goals

It's important to remember that these examples are designed to show what a story-focused social media campaign's output might look like in practice. They are not one-for-one guides that you can apply to your organisation wholecloth. They are aimed at giving you ideas to get you started, but it's always important to relate your own social media actions back to your goals, to measure the results and to take a data-driven approach throughout.

Q&A sessions

Imagine this.

Dewey, Cheatem & Howe (DCH) is a corporate law firm. Their marketing goal is to build the reputation of their lawyers as experts and thought leaders on social media. Their ultimate business goal here is to attract new talent (employees) and enquiries from potential clients (prospects).

To achieve this, the firm has launched a new campaign where one of their top lawyers will answer questions sent in by users via social media. This type of live Q&A is usually called an *Ask Me Anything*, or *AMA*.

The lawyer takes a unique approach to answering the questions by deciding to turn them into stories. Instead of rattling off dry legal advice, she relates her answers to her personal experience in the industry. The advice is still legally sound, but it's also far more engaging.

For example, if she was asked about the challenges of representing a client in a high-profile case, she would share a story about how she worked tirelessly to prepare her client for a deposition that ultimately helped that client win the case.

This approach not only provides valuable insights for DCH's social media followers but also showcases the lawyer's expertise in a more captivating way, making her stand out from her competitors and other Q&A sessions. It's a creative way for DCH to leverage social media to build their reputation and attract new talent and enquiries to the firm.

How does this approach attract talent? By putting personalities front and centre, DCH also has the opportunity to promote their company culture and get would-be employees excited about some of the people they could work with. At the same time, by demonstrating the expertise of their lawyers, DCH can build their reputation among prospects and gain more clients.

Here's an expanded example of how storytelling could be used in a Q&A like this to captivate the audience and help DCH meet its goals:

Question
Our startup is about to close a funding round with investors. Is there anything we need to consider in terms of legal documents and agreements?

Answer
Great question. I remember earlier in my career I had a client that was a fin-tech startup called Pennywise. They were in a very similar position, about to close a funding round with their investors. Sounds great right? Wrong.

The trouble was that they hadn't created a proper shareholders' agreement, so they ended up in deadlock. Without a clear agreement, they were constantly struggling with their shareholders when it came to decision-making. It was a nightmare. With our help they got back on their feet, but it took time.

You need to make sure you have a water-tight agreement with your investors - that means crossing all the Ts and dotting the Is to make sure all documents are clear on your financials, valuation and the rights and responsibilities of both you and your investors. Don't leave anything to chance!

Here's another example. Here, instead of using a real case, they use a very short, simple allegory.

Question

I run a mid-sized manufacturing company and I'm considering acquiring a competitor. Any advice to help the acquisition go smoothly?

Answer

Ever hear the one about the monkey and the peanuts? I had an old mentor who'd tell me all the time. There's a monkey, and he comes across a jar of peanuts. He reaches in without even thinking. What does he get? His hand stuck.

Acquisitions can be exciting, but you've got to plan carefully or you're going to end up in trouble. I've known plenty of businesses that acquire a competitor without the proper due diligence and end up inheriting loads of legal liabilities.

Conduct a thorough due diligence process that involves reviewing you and the company you're going to acquire's financial statements, legal contracts, and intellectual property. Engage in open and transparent communication with them to ensure the acquisition went smoothly and to avoid any future legal disputes. Conducting proper due diligence is crucial to avoid costly legal risks when acquiring a competitor.

Here's a third example where they answer the question by relating it to a true, humorous story from a different industry:

Question

Our company is expanding internationally, and we're not sure how to navigate the different legal systems and regulations. What should we consider before making this move?

Answer

Do you know why the Chevy Nova, the muscle car, didn't sell well in Mexico? In Spanish, Nova means "no go." Going international is full of challenges - you're right to be cautious.

When expanding your business internationally, it is important to be aware of the legal systems and regulations of the new country you are entering. To avoid any legal hurdles and reputational damage, it is crucial to conduct thorough research and engage in open communication with local legal counsel.

By being prepared and working with the right legal resources, you can ensure compliance with local laws and regulations, and anticipate any potential legal risks that may arise. Remember that legal strategies that worked in your home country may not be applicable in a new environment, so it is important to be open to adaptation and willing to adjust your approach accordingly.

Here's an example from another industry, with another approach.

Kehinde works at a public relations agency called WIST. He also runs live Q&As as part of WIST's social media marketing.

However, these Q&As don't answer questions about public relations directly. Instead, Kehinde does "Life at WIST" Q&As aimed at recruiting young people into the PR agency's graduate scheme.

Although the goal and the focus of the Q&A is different to DCH's, Kehinde can also infuse his answers with storytelling techniques to get his audience of potential applicants engaged. Below is an example. Don't be fooled by the simplicity of the question or the personal nature of the answer - creating this kind of relationship and non-corporate-feeling social presence is perfect for meeting this goal.

Question

I'd love to work in PR, but so many businesses are in London and I don't know if I'd be able to afford the rent and cost of living as a new grad. Got any tips or advice?

Answer

I totally get that! When I joined WIST, I was in the same boat, worrying about affording life in the city. It ended up being quite the adventure, and I don't regret it one bit!

First off, you're right: living in London on a budget isn't a walk in the park. But I discovered some tricks that made it work for me. Instead of aiming for those fancy city centre flats, I decided to explore the cool neighbourhoods on the outskirts. I found a cosy little apartment near Wembley, and guess what? It wasn't only well-connected but also much friendlier on my bank account. That's what we call a win-win!

Now, when it comes to money, I've learned to be savvy and keep a watchful eye on my spending. I created a budget and stuck to it religiously. I realised that those small expenses on the weekend can add up in no time, so I made a conscious effort to cut back on unnecessary stuff. Believe me, it made a huge difference in my savings.

But here's a sneaky extra tip I picked up along the way: work perks are like little hidden treasures waiting to be discovered! At WIST, they offer some amazing deals, like discounted travel cards and gym memberships. I'll let you in on a secret – I take full advantage of those goodies. It's not only a great way to save money but also an opportunity to enjoy some well-deserved perks. Trust me, it's totally worth it!

And hey, if you're still feeling the squeeze, let me share one more bit of personal experience with you. Remote work has become more common these days, and it's a game-changer. I've had conversations with my manager about flexible arrangements. This allowed me to find a place a bit outside the pricey London zone, where the rent was more affordable, while still pursuing my dream career in PR. I also don't have to spend money on transport every day.

Don't let the cost of living in London hold you back. With a positive mindset and a few tricks up your sleeve, you can navigate the city, find your perfect spot and make your PR dreams come true without breaking the bank. You've got this!

Promoting thought leadership

The CEO of MovieBox, a film and TV distribution company, is writing a newsletter that will go out on a social media platform.

The aim of the newsletter is to promote articles the team has written on the company's blog to make the team known as thought leaders in their areas of expertise.

The main article that they are promoting for this newsletter was written by their head of marketing, Mark Head, who they want to promote as a thought leader in the marketing world. Mark's article is about how first-hand marketing (i.e. recommendations from friends) is still the most powerful form of marketing for new shows and movies, which is why social media influencers perform so well promoting content compared to traditional advertising.

Below is an example of how the CEO of the business could promote Mark's article by telling a story from their own personal experience that supports the article's main point.

This doesn't have to be a newsletter. It could also be the script for a video that's posted on social media, or a post on a channel that supports and encourages longer-form writing. It could even be broken up into a thread, where each paragraph or so is a different post in the thread.

Here's the example:

Picture this. It was the summer after my secondary school graduation, and I was ready to hit the road with my very first car.

It was a silver VW Polo, and I was over the moon about it. But the truth is, I didn't choose that car because of any expert opinion or extensive research. Nope. I chose it because my best friend had the exact same model, and she swore by its reliability. And you know what? She was right. That car was a faithful companion for years to come.

Fast forward to my last vacation, and I found myself in a similar situation. My partner and I were staying at an Airbnb in a quaint little town, and we were in search of the perfect place to enjoy a glass of wine. That's when our host recommended a nearby wine bar. We decided to give it a try, and it turned out to be exactly what we were looking for. In fact, we ended up going back there several times during our stay.

These experiences got me thinking about the power of word of mouth. Sure, we live in a world of ads and social media, but when it comes down to it, there's nothing quite like a personal recommendation from someone you trust. Think about it. Would you rather trust a search engine's top-rated restaurant or your best friend's opinion?

Are you more likely to watch a new show or movie because you saw it advertised, or because a friend recommended it?

That's where influencers come in.

They know that the best way to promote any product or service is by making it feel like a first-hand recommendation. In his latest article, our Head of Marketing, Mark Head, explores the power of word of mouth and how influencers use it to their advantage. Check it out in the link below and discover we can harness this ancient but effective marketing tactic to your advantage.

Here's another example, this time promoting a different blog post.

I used to think I was invincible. As a teenager, whatever I was faced with, I'd also barrel ahead. I thought that ambition alone would make me succeed.

That changed the day I went rock climbing.

I had signed up for a rock climbing session in Croydon with some friends. As always, I barreled ahead, not looking down. As I ascended higher and higher, I realised that I had underestimated the difficulty of the climb. Panic set in. I looked down, and froze like a deer in headlights.

It was a humbling experience. It taught me that sometimes, taking on new challenges requires me to be realistic about my abilities first.

Fast forward to a recent conversation I had with Hannah, our Managing Director. We talked about the value of "agnostic thinking" and it immediately reminded me of my rock climbing mishap.

Hannah explained that too much ambition can actually hinder progress. Clients may be sceptical of making significant changes to their operations, and a "can't be done" attitude can stifle innovation. That's where her idea of agnostic thinking comes in - it's an open-minded approach that allows for creative solutions to be explored, even if they challenge the status quo.

Consider adopting an agnostic mindset. Think of it like approaching a difficult climb - you may not have all the answers at first, but by approaching the situation with an open mind and a willingness to explore new ideas, you just might find the innovative solutions that you need to make a real difference.

Read all about Hannah's "agnostic thinking" in her new blog post.

Here's a final example. Alicia works for a software firm called Buggy - but that isn't the topic of her thought leadership storytelling on social media. Instead, she releases blog posts and videos about her experience as a neurodivergent woman in her industry.

She shares her experiences online, talks about stigma and the ways her workplace has helped her, and posts from events. In some cases, these events are specifically to do with neurodiversity.

In other cases, Alicia speaks about neurodiversity at broader industry events. Here's an example of a thought leadership blog post Alicia might write, using storytelling to promote herself as a thought leader and, by proxy, the positive company culture at Buggy:

> As a software developer, I'm used to dealing with bugs in code. But when it comes to the challenges of being a neurodiverse woman in the tech industry, there's no easy fix. For a long time, I felt like an outsider, struggling to navigate a workplace that didn't understand my needs.
>
> At my old company, neurodiversity was about as welcome as a power outage at a live demo. The open-plan office was a sensory nightmare, with fluorescent lights and constant chatter. I felt like I was on edge all the time, always searching for a quiet space to escape to.
>
> As a neurodiverse person, I also sometimes find myself struggling with small talk or office banter. I tried my best to fit in, but I often felt like I was missing the punchline.
>
> Things came to a head when I was given a project with a tight deadline. I tried my best to keep up, but the pressure was too much. My productivity suffered, and I missed the deadline. My boss wasn't exactly understanding, and accused me of not putting in enough effort. I was frustrated and felt like my neurodiversity was holding me back.
>
> But then, like a beacon of hope, I found Buggy. This company was different. They didn't just tolerate

neurodiversity, they embraced it. The HR department took the time to understand my needs and provided me with everything I needed to be successful. The quiet workspace, the noise-cancelling headphones, and even the adjusted lighting in my office made all the difference.

But it wasn't just the accommodations that made Buggy stand out. They actively sought out ways to include neurodiverse individuals in the workplace. They organised events and workshops that created a safe space where individuals like me could share our experiences and learn from each other.

But the real game-changer was the training that Buggy provided to its employees. They offered workshops that helped neurotypical individuals understand the challenges that neurodiverse individuals face. They also provided training on how to communicate and work effectively with neurodiverse individuals. The result? A workplace where I felt supported, valued, and included.

I'm grateful to work for a company like Buggy that values and celebrates neurodiversity. They recognized the challenges that neurodiverse individuals face and put specific steps in place to tackle them. And as for me? Things aren't always easy, but now I'm in an environment where being neurodivergent isn't just okay - it's celebrated.

Talent acquisition

You're scrolling through your social media feed, bored and unimpressed by the endless stream of ads and promotions. Suddenly, a post catches your eye.

It's not just a product or service being advertised, but a personal story from someone's life - a story that just happens to be connected to their job. Suddenly, you're interested. You're intrigued. You're inspired. Most importantly, you're interested in applying for a job at that company.

That's the power of turning your attempts to attract new talent on social media into stories. By putting your employees and their experiences at the forefront, you can create a connection with potential candidates that no amount of job listings or company profiles can match.

Below are five examples of companies across different sectors using social media posts to harness the power of employee stories and attract top talent.

Marketing agency:

At Hop Digital, the team's Friday ping pong games have taken on a life of their own.

Emma, the social media strategist, has turned them into an epic saga, complete with rivalries, trash talk, and dramatic comebacks. She films the games, adding her own commentary and editing the footage into short, entertaining clips that get uploaded to the company's social media pages.

These videos showcase the agency's fun, creative culture and attract potential job candidates who are looking for a workplace that values teamwork and having a good time.

Logistics company:

Bolivar Logistics is more than just a place to work - it's a way of life.

Simon, a truck driver at the company, has made his truck into a home away from home, decorating it with all the comforts he needs to make life on the road feel relaxing and enjoyable. In a series of videos and posts, Simon takes viewers on a tour of his truck and shares his tips for staying comfortable and happy while driving.

These stories highlight the unique aspects of working at Bolivar Logistics and appeal to people who crave adventure, independence, and the chance to see new places.

HR consulting firm:

At Hire Ground, the consultants are passionate about helping companies build diverse and inclusive workplaces.

Jessica, a consultant at the firm, shares her own story on social media to show how her personal experiences have influenced her professional values. Through a series of posts and videos, Jessica talks about her upbringing and the role her mother played in shaping her worldview. She also discusses how she uses her position at Hire Ground to help companies create more equitable and welcoming work environments.

These stories showcase the firm's commitment to diversity and inclusion and attract job seekers who want to make a positive impact in the world.

Technology company:

At Ctrl Freak, the team is all about using technology to improve wellbeing.

Melchior, a software engineer at the company, has taken on the role of wellbeing champion, using social media to share tips and resources for staying healthy and happy. He also uses his software expertise to create tools that help the team track their moods and communicate their needs. Through a series of blog posts, videos, and social media updates, Melchior shows how technology can be used to create a more supportive and caring workplace.

These stories attract job seekers who are looking for a company that values employee wellbeing and is committed to using technology for good.

Accounting firm:

Fiscal Fitness is not your typical accounting firm - twice a week our team comes together in a high-end coworking space in the heart of Edinburgh.

Rachel, a tax accountant at the firm, takes viewers on a tour of the office through a series of social media posts. She shows off the stylish decor, the state-of-the-art equipment, and the bustling community of entrepreneurs and creatives who work there.

Rachel's stories highlight the unique environment and culture of Fiscal Fitness, appealing to job seekers who are looking for a workplace that is modern, dynamic, and inspiring.

Promoting events

Here's an example of how storytelling can take event promotion to the next level.

BlackpoolSEO is a conference that brings together experts from across the search engine optimisation industry. Instead of just focusing on what attendees will learn, the social media marketing for the event tells stories about the experiences attendees have had, and can expect to have.

The very first chapter of this book begins with this quote from American writer and activist Maya Angelou: "I've learned that people will forget what you said, people will forget what you did, but people will never forget how you made them feel." That absolutely applies here.

To showcase the event experience, BlackpoolSEO organisers release videos featuring attendees chatting and laughing, walking excitedly into event halls, and enjoying the various events and parties that go on each evening. By sharing this content on social media, they're inviting others to be part of the fun and excitement.

But that's not all. The organisers also share the story of BlackpoolSEO itself - how it started with just 10 industry experts renting a room above a pub and has now grown to become the biggest event in the city. By sharing this story, they're showing attendees that they're part of something special and that the conference has come a long way.

When promoting an event, it's important to focus on the experience you'll create for attendees and share the story of how the event came to be. By doing so, you'll not only pique people's interest but also create a sense of community and excitement around your event. Don't just tell stories, leave your audience thinking about the stories they'll be able to tell after they've been to the event.

Technical writing

Storytelling can help you or members of your team promote their technical expertise on social media, while keeping their content engaging. Here's how:

> Stop someone on the street and ask them what they think when they hear "AI."
>
> You'll likely hear a few answers. ChatGPT. Automation. Computers taking over the human race.
>
> Many conversations about AI are warped by preconceptions. These range from sci-fi ideas about AI capabilities, to limited understandings of AI's use based on specific services.
>
> Artificial intelligence plays a vital role in Google Analytics 4.
>
> Forget ChatGPT and forget science-fiction. To understand AI's role in GA4, you need to understand exactly what Google is using it for, and how it can help you.

Lead generation

You can use the power of storytelling to win more work directly. You can also use the power of storytelling to promote the work you've already done to (you guessed it) win even more work.

Turning the positive experiences of your previous and current clients into stories is a great way to attract new clients. Take a look at this example from a marketing agency:

> Audience research and customer insight is a critical part of any successful digital marketing activity.
>
> In 2022, Face Creative undertook a project to rebuild Capital City Airport's website to reflect its values and improve revenue generation.
>
> To design the new website, it was vital that we first gain an exhaustive understanding of all of the needs of Capital City Airport's passengers. This didn't just mean understanding the airport experience at large. Our goal was to understand the nuances of the passenger experience at Capital City Airport in particular, from the layout and amenities to transport and security.
>
> That's why we became passengers.

What follows is a case study explaining how the different observations about the customer experience at the airport informed the design of the site itself. Unlike a normal case study, however, this focuses on experiences and events rather than just outcomes, allowing the company to promote its people and process as well as its results. By using storytelling to show how something was done, not just that it was done, the business can give prospective clients more confidence that the results in this case weren't just luck but were the result of the personalities and processes involved - which they will get too, if they hire the agency.

Here is another example, this time from a commercial property company.

Top Prop Commercial Properties knows that sharing expertise and insights with its audience is a powerful way to generate leads and engage potential clients. Through their monthly newsletter, Top Prop delivers valuable information on market conditions, trending locations, industry trends, and the impact of workplace culture on where people choose to work.

In each newsletter, Top Prop incorporates storytelling to captivate readers and make the content more relatable. Let's take a look at a recent example:

> Subject: Unveiling London's Dynamic Property Landscape: A Journey Through the Capital's Vibrant Districts
>
> Dear [Name],
>
> London, a city of timeless charm and captivating diversity, offers a thriving property market that never ceases to amaze. At Top Prop, we take pride in providing you with

exclusive insights to help navigate this dynamic landscape. Join us on a journey through the capital's vibrant districts, where opportunities abound for those seeking prime real estate ventures.

A Cultural Renaissance: Shoreditch and the East End

Once an industrial hub, Shoreditch and the surrounding East End have undergone a remarkable transformation, evolving into a cultural hotspot that blends innovation, creativity, and heritage. Step into the bustling streets and explore the stories of pioneering entrepreneurs, innovative start-ups, and captivating street art. Delve into the rich history and witness how this district has become a magnet for young professionals and trendsetters alike.

The Riverside Revival: Exploring South Bank's Urban Renaissance

Nestled along the Thames, South Bank has emerged as a symbol of urban revitalisation. Through the lens of renowned architects and passionate urban planners, we unveil the secrets behind the district's metamorphosis. Immerse yourself in a world of iconic landmarks, vibrant festivals, and cultural institutions that have breathed new life into this riverside neighbourhood, making it a sought-after destination for residential and commercial investments alike.

The Green Oasis: Sustainability and Property Development in Canary Wharf

Canary Wharf, synonymous with towering skyscrapers and bustling financial activity, has embraced a new identity as a sustainable urban enclave. Join us as we delve into the ambitious sustainability initiatives, lush green spaces, and eco-conscious architecture that are transforming this iconic business district. Discover how Canary Wharf harmonises corporate success with environmental responsibility, attracting forward-thinking businesses and environmentally conscious investors.

We hope you've enjoyed this month's edition of Top Prop's Insights. If you've made it this far, we would love to hear from you!

Use the hashtag #TopProp to share your thoughts on social media. Your engagement helps us tailor our content to your interests and provide you with even more valuable insights in the future.

Stay tuned for our next edition, where we'll unravel the untapped potential of more exciting London districts!

Best regards,

The Top Prop Team

By infusing storytelling with expert knowledge, Top Prop crafts a newsletter that not only educates but also resonates with their audience's aspirations. The inclusion of a call-to-action at the end, inviting readers to engage further, helps identify the most interested individuals and allows Top Prop to nurture these leads. By building relationships through storytelling, Top Prop can attract new clients and establish their authority in London's competitive property market.

Influencers and brand ambassadors

As we covered back in the chapter *Influencing Influencers*, influencers are master storytellers.

Here's how an influencer might talk about a brand at the end of a video or in a post promoting a graphic design service, using storytelling to engage their audience:

> My daughter is an amazing artist.
>
> She's so much better than me that it's almost embarrassing - and she's five years old. I mean, I can barely draw a stick figure. Take a look at this picture she drew last week.
>
> Compare that to this picture to this drawing I did at the same age that my mum still has on her fridge. It's a mess, to be honest. The sun is way too large, the sky is only blue at the top. This guy's legs are half the length of his body. Horrible.
>
> But you know what? It's special. It's a reminder of the times when I was just starting out as a creator, trying to find my own style and voice. I just needed a little help.
>
> That's where Sketch Solutions comes in. They're an absolute lifesaver for people like me who may not have a natural talent for art but still want to express themselves creatively. With their help, I've been able to turn my ideas

into stunning visuals across all my channels that capture the essence of who I am.

Whether you're an artist at heart or not, don't worry. Sketch Solutions has got you covered.

Trust me, it'll be a game-changer.

Here's another example. Bev is an influencer who has also become a thought leader and has leveraged that to start and promote her business.

Bursting with infectious energy, Bev began her journey as an influencer by capturing the hearts and minds of her followers through her enthusiastic activewear reviews, sweat-inducing gym routines and workout tips. The fitness community on social media video platforms couldn't get enough of her motivational spirit, and she quickly ascended the ranks of influencer stardom.

But she wasn't content with basking in the spotlight. Bev had a grand vision in mind—to change the game for the entire fitness industry. With a daring pivot, she unleashed her creativity and entrepreneurial spirit, venturing into uncharted territory. She launched her own sustainable activewear line, GreenFit. Bev saw an opportunity to merge her passion for fitness with her unwavering commitment to the planet, and seized it with unbridled enthusiasm.

GreenFit line became the talk of social media's fitness community - a blend of style, comfort, and eco-consciousness that struck a chord with her dedicated following. Bev had not only built an empire but also set a shining example for others in the industry, proving that fashion and sustainability could coexist.

With a natural gift for social media storytelling, Bev wove her narrative, inviting aspiring entrepreneurs into her world. She revealed the secrets of her success, peeled back the layers of running a business, and fearlessly tackled the challenges faced by women in the industry. Her wisdom became a beacon of light for those navigating the treacherous waters of entrepreneurship, empowering them to chase their dreams and defy the odds.

Bev's journey from a fitness influencer to a thought leader and businesswoman shows the boundless possibilities that lie within the realm of storytelling. Through her audacious pivots, unyielding passion, and a commitment to making a positive impact, Bev redefined what it means to be an influencer. She shattered expectations.

By building her audience as an influencer, the creation and success of Bev's fitness brand becomes a story in and of itself, just like the one above. It's also fueled by storytelling opportunities every step of the way. Bev's original fitness videos, for example, could take the form of day-in-the-life stories which show off her routine. The launch of GreenFit could be promoted as the next chapter of her story on her social media. Eventually, her entire story might be picked up by the media and written up like in the example text above.

ESG content

ESG - environment, social and governance - is focused on the positive impact your organisation is having. Here are three examples of how different businesses could promote their ESG efforts with social media storytelling.

EverGreen is a software development company, dedicated to combating climate change and promoting environmental sustainability in their industry. They have implemented several initiatives to lead by example and reduce their carbon footprint. By adopting renewable energy sources, optimising energy consumption, and developing eco-friendly software solutions, they're tackling the environmental challenges associated with the technology sector. Not only do they publish all this in an annual sustainability report, they also share that report across social media with an added element of storytelling:

> We recently asked a group of school students at South Croydon Primary School to share their thoughts on what Britain would look like in 100 years time.
>
> One theme came up time and again. They envisioned a greener, more sustainable Britain. They painted pictures of cities adorned with lush green spaces, renewable energy and thriving eco-friendly transport. The next generation hopes for a Britain where there is a harmony between technology and the environment.

At EverGreen, we were inspired by their belief in the possibility of a sustainable world. It reminded us why we work every day to make a difference through our software solutions and environmental initiatives.

Today, we proudly share our Annual Sustainability Report—a testament to our commitment to environmental responsibility. In its pages, you'll discover how we're reducing our carbon footprint, embracing renewable energy sources and developing eco-friendly software solutions that empower businesses to operate sustainably. It's a story of transformation and impact - a story we invite you to be a part of.

[Link to the Annual Sustainability Report]

This story could also be told as a video compiling clips of the students talking about their hopes for the future, promoting the report in the description. What's important is that EverGreen isn't just doing fantastic work, they're able to get the word out there about that work and get more businesses onboard. Here's a second example.

Sentry is a company that manufactures large machinery for use in other industries. The business has a long-standing commitment to social responsibility and community well-being. Leadership prioritises employee welfare, fair labour practices and actively engaging with the communities they work in. Through their innovative industrial equipment, they aim to address infrastructure development challenges and contribute to disaster relief efforts, fostering resilience and progress. To promote these efforts through storytelling, the marketing team has put together a video interviewing different Sentry employees in their workplaces, putting those employees' stories front and centre.

Here is what the transcript of that video could look like:

> [Video opens with upbeat music and scenes of workers operating machinery. The screen transitions to an interview-style setup with a Sentry employee.]
>
> Nik - Quality Control Specialist: "Hi, I'm Nik, and I've been part of the Sentry family for five years. Last year, we partnered with a local school to provide STEM education resources, inspiring the next generation of engineers and innovators."
>
> [Cut to scenes of Nik interacting with colleagues and footage of Sentry employees engaging with students.]
>
> Mark - Production Supervisor: "I'm Mark, the Production Supervisor at Sentry. Our leadership team places a strong emphasis on employee welfare and fair labour practices. It's not just words; they take real action. We recently implemented a flexible work schedule that allows our team members to balance work and personal responsibilities more effectively."
>
> [Cut to scenes of Mark overseeing production and Sentry employees enjoying flexible work arrangements.]
>
> Lisa - Human Resources Coordinator: "Hey there, I'm Lisa, the Human Resources Coordinator at Sentry. Taking care of our employees is essential to creating a positive

work environment. Our company invests in employee development programs, offering training opportunities to enhance skills and open up career pathways within the company."

[Cut to scenes of Lisa organising training programs and employees participating in workshops.]

James - Machine Operator: "I'm James, a dedicated Machine Operator at Sentry. One of the things that truly sets us apart is our active involvement in the communities where we operate. When flooding struck our neighbouring town last year, our team quickly mobilised and provided our machinery to assist in the rebuilding efforts, helping the community get back on its feet."

[Cut to scenes of James operating machinery and footage of Sentry equipment being used in disaster-stricken areas.]

Emma - Project Manager: "Hi, I'm Emma, a Project Manager at Sentry. Our innovative industrial equipment not only addresses infrastructure development challenges but also creates lasting impacts. We recently completed a large-scale project that improved transportation infrastructure, reducing commute times for thousands of people and boosting the local economy."

[Cut to scenes of Emma overseeing projects and footage of Sentry machinery being used in construction sites.]

Carlos - Assembly Technician: "I'm Carlos, an experienced Assembly Technician at Sentry. It's incredibly fulfilling to work for a company that actively engages in disaster relief efforts. Last year, we collaborated with a non-profit organisation to provide our machinery for free to regions affected by natural disasters, helping communities rebuild and recover."

[Cut to scenes of Carlos assembling machinery and footage of Sentry equipment being used in disaster-stricken areas.]

[Throughout the video, different employees passionately share specific examples of Sentry's positive social impact, showcasing the company's commitment to social responsibility and community well-being.]

[The video concludes with scenes of employees celebrating their accomplishments together.]

On-screen text: "Sentry: Empowering our workforce, uplifting communities, and shaping a brighter future."

[End of video]

Ok - you can do better. The point is to get employees telling their own stories about the positive impact they've been able to make working with Sentry, and the positive impact the company's practices have had on them.

Here's a third example.

Ethica is a challenger bank dedicated to exemplary governance practices, transparency, and responsible investment strategies within the financial industry. They prioritise maintaining the highest standards of integrity to build trust and stability for their clients. Through rigorous internal controls, compliance frameworks and responsible investment decisions, the bank aims to address ethical concerns and contribute to a healthier financial ecosystem. There's only one problem - the governance systems of a bank aren't exactly exciting. That's where storytelling comes in.

Here's an example of a post Ethica could roll out on social media:

> Meet Sara, a passionate social entrepreneur who had a brilliant idea to address environmental challenges in her community. She dreamt of creating a sustainable energy project that would provide clean, renewable power to underserved areas. However, like many innovators, Sara faced significant barriers when it came to securing funding for her ambitious project.
>
> That's where Ethica stepped in.
>
> Our dedicated team recognised Sara's vision and the positive change it could bring. We understood that traditional banks might not fully grasp the potential of her venture, but at Ethica, we have a different approach. By leveraging our expertise in responsible investment decisions, we saw the alignment between Sara's project and our commitment to creating a healthier financial ecosystem.
>
> Through transparent discussions and rigorous due diligence, Ethica provided Sara with the financial support she needed to turn her dream into a reality. Our responsible investment strategies ensured that her project

not only benefited the environment but also had a sound financial footing. With Ethica's backing, Sara's sustainable energy project flourished, bringing clean energy and economic opportunities to countless lives.

At Ethica, we are committed to nurturing long-term relationships with our clients. We continue to provide guidance and support to Sara as her project grows, helping her navigate the ever-evolving landscape of sustainable finance. We believe in the power of collaboration and knowledge sharing, and through our ongoing partnership with Sara, we are collectively driving positive change in the world.

Sara's story is just one of many that illustrate the immense impact ethical banking can have on individuals, communities, and the planet. By prioritising integrity, responsible investment decisions, and transparent governance, Ethica is transforming the banking industry, one client at a time.

Investor relations

When managing the relationship your business has with its investors, you can't just rely on reporting the facts. You need to turn them into a digestible, engaging story.

Here's an example of the CEO statement that a TV channel could use to kick off its annual report to its investors:

> VisionTV isn't just meant to entertain. Since our founding in 1983, our mission has been to inspire positive change in society.
>
> Our award-winning documentary series, "Voices Unheard", highlights the unheard voices of marginalised communities and individuals. From exploring the struggles of refugees and asylum seekers to shining a light on the experiences of those living with disabilities, we are committed to representing the diversity of the United Kingdom and elevating emerging writers, producers, and individuals from marginalised communities.
>
> Our political talk show, "Power Play", takes on the powerful and holds them accountable. From scrutinising politicians' policies and actions to calling out big corporations for unethical practices, we don't just challenge for the sake of it, but to push boundaries, question conventions, and inspire reflection and critical thought.

But we don't stop there. At VisionTV, we are constantly seeking to reinvent entertainment. Our reality TV show, "Making a Difference", puts the spotlight on ordinary people who are making extraordinary contributions to society. We aim to discover and develop new talent, find new ways to engage with our audiences, and build new partnerships to create content that is not only entertaining but also impactful and meaningful.

Through our TV programs, we have created a profound impact on society, our viewers, British culture, the creative industries, and the wider economy. We are proud to be a unique and distinct entity, with a vision for a better world. Be part of the change with VisionTV.

User-generated content

Storytelling is one of the most powerful tools we have as humans. We love sharing our experiences and hearing the experiences of others. It's in our DNA. If you don't agree by now, you're probably reading this book back-to-front.

Tapping into this innate desire to share stories can be a game-changer. If you can find ways to get your audience to share their own stories on social media, you'll be well on your way to increasing engagement and achieving your goals.

Here's an example scenario:

Meet Amina, a skilled consultant who knows a thing or two about delivering compelling presentations. In a video, Amina shares some tips and ideas to help people improve their presentation skills.

But instead of simply asking for likes and shares, she takes a different approach. Amina poses a question to her viewers: "Have you ever had to pull a presentation out of the bag too? Let me know in the comments below!"

By asking this question, Amina not only invites people to engage with their content, but she also prompts them to share their own stories. And as we've established, people love to share stories!

One viewer might respond with a story about how he had to improvise during a presentation when his PowerPoint wouldn't work. He ended up giving a talk without any visuals, and it turned out to be one of his best presentations ever.

Another viewer might share a story about how she was nervous before a big presentation and how she overcame that nervousness by practising in front of a mirror.

Yet another viewer might tell a story about how they had to give a presentation in a foreign language, and how they had to rely on their charisma and storytelling skills to connect with the audience.

These are just a few examples of the types of stories that people might share in response to Amina's question. By encouraging her viewers to share their experiences, she's not only increasing engagement with her content, but she's also building a sense of community around a shared experience. So next time you're creating content, think about how you can use storytelling to engage your audience and create a sense of connection.

Here's another example.

Lawn Rangers is a company that sells gardening products. They send out free sunflower seed packets with every order. Customers are encouraged to plant the seeds and share their sunflowers' progress on social media with a specific hashtag so that Lawn Rangers can follow their progress.

For every plant that grows over 30cm tall, Lawn Rangers plants a tree. The company also shares these stories on social media to raise awareness.

Here's an example of a simple post Lawn Rangers might share on social media:

Say hello to Jane, one of our super-talented and eco-conscious customers! When Jane received her Lawn Rangers order, she was overjoyed to find a free packet of sunflower seeds inside. Being a total gardening enthusiast and an eco-warrior, she immediately decided to take on the #LawnRangersGrow challenge.

Jane planted her sunflower seeds in a raised garden bed in her back garden and poured all her love, care, and expertise into them. She diligently documented her progress on social media using our hashtag, #LawnRangersGrow, and kept us all on the edge of our seats with every post.

Finally, after weeks of hard work, Jane's sunflowers had reached over 40cm tall! She couldn't contain her excitement!

But Jane's impact didn't end there. Thanks to her dedication and hard work, Lawn Rangers has been able to plant dozens of trees across the country. For every sunflower that grows over 30cm tall, we plant a tree. It's our way of giving back to the environment and promoting sustainable living.

We're incredibly proud of Jane and all of our customers who have embraced the #LawnRangersGrow challenge! So, whether you're a seasoned green thumb or a budding gardener, be sure to check out our selection of high-quality gardening products and join the #LawnRangersGrow community. Share your progress with us on social media using the hashtag #LawnRangersGrow, and let's grow together!

Here's another example. "Tech Management Innovations" (TMI) is a leading software development company specialising in cutting-edge solutions for businesses in various industries.

TMI recently launched a groundbreaking software platform designed to revolutionise inventory management for retailers. To promote their product, they decide to leverage the power of storytelling to engage with their target audience.

In a blog post titled *Retail Chronicles: Unforgettable Inventory Mishaps* TMI shares a collection of stories submitted by retailers who have encountered challenging inventory situations in the past. By doing so, they not only entertain their audience but also create a sense of empathy and community among retailers facing similar issues. Here are some of the stories:

Emma's Inventory Triumph

As the owner of a small clothing boutique, I take pride in delivering exceptional customer experiences. However, one day, my store was hit by an unexpected surge in customers, leading to a rapid depletion of inventory. Panic set in as I realised my inventory management system was failing to keep up with the overwhelming demand. At that moment, I knew I had to think on my feet and find a solution to ensure a seamless shopping experience for my valued customers.

With time ticking away, my eyes landed on a nearby display rack adorned with the latest collection of accessories. A surge of inspiration flooded through me. I swiftly repurposed the display rack to hold extra inventory, transforming it into a makeshift storage solution. Carefully arranging and organising the garments, I replenished the depleted racks on the shop floor.

To my delight, my quick thinking paid off as the customers continued to pour into my boutique. The repurposed display rack allowed them to browse and select their desired items without any disruption. Seeing their satisfaction and appreciation for my resourcefulness was incredibly rewarding. It was a moment that solidified my belief in the power of thinking outside the box and finding creative solutions to unexpected challenges.

James and the Holiday Delivery Mishap

As the operations manager of a bustling supermarket chain, my responsibility is to ensure that our stores are well-stocked and ready to meet the needs of our customers. However, just before a major holiday weekend, disaster struck. A crucial delivery, containing essential items that our customers eagerly awaited for their celebrations, encountered unforeseen delays. The realisation of a potential shortage during such a critical period sent shockwaves through our operation.

I could feel the weight of the situation on my shoulders as I knew the disappointment it could bring to our loyal shoppers. Gathering my team, we knew we had to find a solution swiftly. We brainstormed ideas, fueled by a collective sense of urgency, to redirect inventory from other store locations and fill the impending void.

Working tirelessly, we devised a temporary system to shuttle the much-needed items from nearby stores. Coordinating with logistics personnel, orchestrating swift transfers, and ensuring the inventory reached our supermarket shelves in time for our customers' demands became our top priority.

Despite the chaos and heightened stress, our relentless efforts paid off. The supermarket remained fully stocked, and our customers could find the essential items they sought for their holiday festivities. The seamless execution of the temporary inventory redirection left our customers blissfully unaware of the behind-the-scenes scramble.

Receiving accolades from both my team and the supermarket chain's leadership, I felt a profound sense of pride. The tale of triumph and resilience during that holiday delivery mishap served as a reminder of our unwavering commitment to customer satisfaction and our ability to overcome even the most challenging situations.

TMI encourages their audience to share their own unforgettable inventory mishaps by leaving comments on the blog post or engaging on social media using the hashtag #RetailChronicles.

They also promise to select a few standout stories and feature them in an upcoming webinar where industry experts will discuss strategies for overcoming inventory challenges.

The response from retailers is overwhelming. Retailers from various backgrounds and experiences enthusiastically share their stories, using the hashtag #RetailChronicles to connect with one another and engage in conversations about inventory management best practices.

TMI carefully curates the stories they receive and compiles them into a series of engaging social media posts. Each post highlights a different retailer's tale and provides a brief summary of the inventory challenge faced and the creative solution implemented. By featuring these stories, TMI not only demonstrates their deep understanding of the industry but also positions themselves as a trusted partner that empathises with retailers' struggles and offers effective solutions.

As the #RetailChronicles campaign gains traction, and more retailers are drawn to TMI's innovative software platform, recognising the company's commitment to addressing their specific pain points. The engagement and participation of retailers create a vibrant online community centred around inventory management, where retailers can exchange advice, insights, and success stories.

TMI's storytelling approach not only boosts engagement and brand awareness but also establishes them as thought leaders in the industry. By genuinely connecting with their audience through relatable stories, they have successfully positioned themselves as a trusted partner for retailers seeking to optimise their inventory management processes.

So, the next time you're brainstorming ways to engage your B2B audience, consider the power of storytelling. Find captivating narratives that resonate with your target market, encourage them to share their own experiences, and build a thriving community around your brand.

Never forget that in the realm of marketing, stories have the power to captivate, connect, and ultimately drive business success.

CLOSING & THANKS

So what's next?

When we started writing this book, we were determined to make sure it wasn't about quick fixes.

Our goal was to help you understand the storytelling principles and steps you need to take to launch your social media marketing strategy and start winning more work. It's a marathon, not a sprint.

That means you can get started right away - start telling stories, start collecting data, start learning and start winning work. The more stories you tell the better storyteller you'll become. The more posts you put out there, the more data you'll have. The best time to start is today.

Looking for help from us?

Reach out at hello@basecreative.co.uk

References

A. https://nealschaffer.com/social-media-marketing-statistics/

B. https://animoto.com/blog/news/social-video-trends-marketers-2020

C. https://en.wikipedia.org/wiki/Oxo_(food)#Marketing

D. https://en.wikipedia.org/wiki/Gold_Blend_couple

1. https://journals.sagepub.com/doi/10.1177/0956797614536401

2. https://www.visualstorytell.com/blog/why-do-we-love-stories

3. https://flsplus.medium.com/why-we-love-storytellers-77ab571b6817

4. https://www.health.harvard.edu/mind-and-mood/oxytocin-the-love-hormone

5. Richard B. Lee & Richard Daly, "Introduction: Foragers & Others," in: The Cambridge Encyclopedia of Hunters & Gatherers (Cambridge University Press, 1999)

6. https://en.wikipedia.org/wiki/Attempts_to_ban_football_games

7. https://www.bl.uk/collection-items/the-anatomy-of-abuses-by-philip-stubbes-1583

8. https://www.dailymail.co.uk/news/article-2075065/More-people-died-playing-football-SWORD-FIGHTING-Tudor-times.html

9. https://irishtechnews.ie/the-psychology-behind-social-media-likes/

Acknowledgements

All material and the people that have helped and inspired us:

- *Chase One Rabbit*, David Parrish
- *Obviously Awesome*, April Dunford
- *Hooked on You*, Ian Harris
- *Pitch Anything*, Oren Klaff
- *They Ask You Answer*, Marcus Sheridan
- *Where Stellar Messages Come From*, Joanna Wiebe
- The team and speakers at BrightonSEO
- Luke Pearce

Thank You

A big thank you for taking the time to read *Socialise*.

Remember, keep a copy somewhere close. You may want to come back to remind yourself of some of the ideas, or you may have an hour or two to spare and are ready to take another step (or leap) forward with your social media marketing.

We'd love to hear your feedback, so please do get in touch with us and let us know. All our details are below - we look forward to hearing from you.

Iain Scott: **linkedin.com/in/iaingscott**

Rebecca Holloway: **linkedin.com/in/beccasocial**

Charlie Stewart: **linkedin.com/in/charlieastewart**

Printed in Great Britain
by Amazon